PARISH
AS
LEARNING COMMUNITY

Modeling for Parish and Adult Growth

by
Tom Downs

PAULIST PRESS
New York/Ramsey/Toronto

Library of Congress
Catalog Card Number: 78-70816

ISBN: 0-8091-2172-7

Published by Paulist Press
Editorial Office: 1865 Broadway, New York, N.Y. 10023
Business Office: 545 Island Road, Ramsey, N.J. 07446

Printed and bound in the
United States of America

Contents

*To Bishop Thomas Grady
and the priests of the Orlando
Diocese,
and my colleagues in the
National Conference of Diocesan
Directors,
all of whom so generously
support me in my ministry*

Introduction

In these pages I welcome the reader to a consideration of some of the dynamics that seem to go into adult learning in the local church. The local church usually takes form and life in the parish, the place where people meet and church happens. Unfortunately, as Hans Kung points out, "church" is often used abstractly and ideally to describe the universal, institutional church in which a specific congregation or parish is only a subdivision,

> . . . as though the Church were not *wholly* present in every place, endowed with the *entire* promise of the Gospel and *entire* faith, recipient of the undivided grace of the Father, having present in it an *undivided* Christ and enriched by the *undivided* Holy Spirit. No, the local Church does not merely belong to the Church, the local Church *is* the Church. The whole Church can only be understood in terms of the local Church and its concrete actions.[1]

Herein I struggle with the challenge of becoming church as part of the *real* parish communities in which we live and for which we are responsible—the places where we consistently gather for initiation, reconciliation and Eucharist, for the preaching of the Word and the sharing of conversation, gifts, learning, caring, charisms, ministries and much else. It is in the parish where the challenge of church occurs in most of our lives. In this community of faith we work out our salvation.

Yet this community is a *human* community, a gathering of people who seek to share and care. Working with each other in this human condition is how our faith comes to light and life. I believe that in our parishes we need to do much better with each other simply as human beings if we are to expect greater freedom and openness to the power and presence of the Spirit in our midst. We live in a modern age and culture where the challenge of becoming human is at the core of our lives. The human skills needed to live creatively and happily with other human beings in a local parish are frequently lacking in our church, even though we know that our lives are changing spiritually only if changing humanly.

To change, of course, is to learn, as to learn is to change. And so the local church becomes, in at least one of its dimensions, a lifelong learning community. The phrase "lifelong learning" is now in vogue. Most everyone, upon reflection, concurs that learning is natural and necessary throughout one's lifetime, from toddling to tottering. "Continue in what you have learned and have firmly believed, knowing from whom you have learned it and how from childhood you have been acquainted with the sacred writings which are able to instruct you for salvation through faith in Jesus Christ" (2 Tim. 3:14-15).

The parish is a role model for the adults that form that community. The very life and mission of the parish provide the primary model for adult growth. A parish in healthy change is the catalyst for adults in healthy change. And conversely, changing adults are the essential basis for changing parishes. One cannot happen without the other. And thus we have very simply the case for lifelong learning as an integral and essential dynamic for healthy parishes. Lifelong learning and a maturing parish—each is crucial to the other.

I wish to deal with these matters in theory, and I do so without apology to those who appreciate the practical. I hope to demonstrate that just as there is nothing so practical as good theory, so there is nothing so theoretical as good practice. Theory is crucial to any significant enterprise in social and cultural systems. In the local parish there is all too little theory and theorizing, and as a result all too much ignorance about what does and what might go on there.

And so in the first chapter I propose a theory of theory-building. Specifically I encourage the use of "models" and "modeling." While some readers may wish to move immediately past this section into a theoretical summary of parish, I think it is important to grasp clearly what is meant when we talk about using models in theology and education, in theory and practice.

In the second and third chapters I offer a review of some *theoretical* models which are used to describe the local parish and adult learners holistically. These help provide a vision of what is implied in a discussion of church and person, and offer as well some categories or "handles" for us to better dialogue about our visions.

How we can better understand and prepare for healthy change in both parishes and persons is presented in terms of *experimental* or change models in chapters four and five. These models suggest how to

create healthy-change-opportunities for Christians
both in parish life (the contextual dimension) and in
formal programs (the programmatic dimension).[2]

In a final chapter I will report briefly on a series of
critical issues discerned and developed by a national
task force on adult education. These issues relate to
lifelong learning in the local parish and exemplify several areas in need of ongoing inquiry, research and
theory.

My hope is that these deliberations will prove helpful to my colleagues in parish life and leadership—
whether adult learners, lay leaders, religious, priests,
professional adult educators or directors of religious
education. I especially wish to supportively challenge
those priests, professional and lay leaders who are most
committed to collaboratively building up the Body of
Christ in these very challenging times. I do not know
that I have a fix on the answers to this challenge, but I
have found that the following discussion provides at
least a helpful direction for us to search out together.

Several colleagues have personally stimulated and
enriched me in this inquiry, and I do thank them
genuinely, viz., Avery Dulles, Robert Hoeffner, Malcolm Knowles, Maurice Monette, James Schaefer,
Thomas Tewey and Emmet Weber. I acknowledge a
special debt of gratitude to my diocese of Orlando and
bishop, Thomas Grady, and the many parishes, priests
and people where I have been taught by the brazen
reality of their situations. And finally I express immense gratitude to my Protestant colleagues who con-
stitute *Creative Interchange Consultants—Florida
Network*, a community of fellow learners and O.D.
consultants who have cared a great deal about church,
and about me.

My wife Bernice has typed several drafts of this manuscript, correcting and improving each time. Thanks to her, and the patience of my children, Anne, Michael and Sara, this project has satisfactorily come to completion.

1
MODELS
AND MODELING

"Models" are on the tip of the tongue of most every leader concerned with change these days. In most arenas of life wise change agents do not proceed in new directions until they have somehow assessed existing reality and measured expected results, just as an architect surveys the property and models the building with blueprints and drawings before construction. From Christ's promise of a "kingdom" to Kennedy's proposal of a "new frontier," from a simple outline drawn by a hand in the sand to a mock-up of a futuristic space craft, models seem to both describe what is and what could be.

Very simply a model is a symbol of a complex reality. Chinese images from the 27th century B.C. and Egyptian hieroglyphics even earlier are ancient examples of models used to describe our universe. Today even our children use models in drawing stick figures to depict people in the world around them. These symbolic representations do not contain all the data and variables known, but only those considered most important to the observer.

A model can simplify a reality so that one can, as it were, get a hold of it in some fashion, understand and communicate it. The more complex the reality, the more necessary the model. For a six year old girl a "stick figure" picture of dad sufficiently simplifies a very mysterious being so that she can better understand and communicate about him.

Models also seem to energize both sides of our personalities. Creating a model challenges the "right" or rationalistic side of personality, which stores an immense amount of abstract data, to focus in on specific items or dimensions of that data. Without this rational harnessing, what I understand and know about something will be so extensive and so complex that my rational system would short out from data-overload. Similarly the "left" or imaginative side of personality is stimulated by models and modeling to go beyond what I know, beyond the limits of immediate experience and logical understanding to see the unseen and unsuspected.

Models are simple but sophisticated representations of some reality that make it possible to both grasp and transcend that reality. Whether a "billiard ball model" to explain low energy phenomena in the physical sciences, or a geo-social grid describing the geographical and sociological qualities of a certain region, the model makes it possible to grasp and express the unexpressible, and deal with it.

Modeling and model-building are simply the use of models, strategies for the interpretation and understanding of complex realities.[3] Modeling has come to us through the physical and social sciences, and has by now become a fruitful resource in theology.[4]

I distinguish *theoretical* and *experimental* models. Theoretical models are more abstract and symbolic representations of reality. They are holistic, seeking to describe the whole rather than the parts, the forest rather than the trees. Theoretical models integrate the wisdom of the more intuitive Eastern philosophies with the logical abstractions of Western philosophy. For this reason theoretical models are "to be taken seriously but not literally."[5]

Experimental models, on the other hand, describe and delineate the trees rather than the forest, the parts rather than the whole. They are more practical and experiential, more concrete and specific. Usually experimental models offer concrete specifications, proposals or courses of action rather than general symbolic overviews of the matter.

For this reason theoretical models are usually devised and designed to understand and explain a profound reality, while experimental models are used to actually and specifically change and alter it. Or to put it differently, theoretical models are utilized to generate theory, while experimental models translate good theory into action or practice.[6] I observe and listen to complex reality with the help of theoretical models; I respond or act upon some part of the world with experimental models.

While this discussion and distinction may seem to take us awry, it will become evident throughout this work that models, especially those we use in theology and education, cannot be used indiscriminately. In these days when the popularity of the social sciences has brought the phenomenon of models into almost every human enterprise, the temptation is to translate almost everything that is or should be into a model, and use models rather glibly and carelessly.

In ecclesiology—the theology of church—models

such as Dulles' "models of the Church" are theoretical and not experimental models. That is to say, they are meant to be "explanatory and exploratory" descriptions of the church. These five models (which we will review in the following chapter) offer an integrated, holistic, theoretical representation of the church in all her depth and mystery. Note they are not separated, partial, experimental representations of the church. The church cannot be understood by any one of the models alone, but only by all of them together. Many people will talk today about a parish being or becoming a "community" (i.e., assimilating the community model of church) as if that were all there is to being church.

Or some will espouse the servant model as the paradigm for a parish and organize the entire parish around the mission of the church to serve the poor and oppressed, as if this were all that a local church is to be. Here again a theoretical model has been misused as an experimental model, and while whatever implementation of the servant model that occurs is commendable, the parish in its other dimensions becomes empty and sterile. The trees have become the forest.

Equally problematical is a misunderstanding of experimental models in theology and education. For example in youth ministry programming I know of a school model, family model, counseling model, retreat model, socialization model, sacramental model, social action model, peer ministry model, and many more. Now these are practical and particular descriptions of how ministry to youth in the church might proceed. If taken as theoretical models, as integrated, complete and holistic descriptions of the matter, they become more than they are meant to be. They run the risk of becoming the whole, the answer, the only way to proceed, the only tree in the forest. Or because they are not whole, they soon prove to be empty and powerless, limited and opaque, readily blown this or that way by whatever wind.

Theoretical models and experimental models are very important for each other, and in fact are of little benefit to humankind without each other. While theoretical models may serve well to grasp and articulate the imponderable, they are rather powerless in the course of human development until or unless they can be translated into precise courses of action or specific products and results. And similarly if experimental models do not have their roots and reference points firmly fixed in theoretical models, they may become defective and dangerous despite the fact that they are effective and successful, or perhaps even because of their success. Only those experimental models which are generated from theoretical models seem to assure authentically and consistently improved versions of the future.

Model-building is the development of theoretical and experimental models *in relationship to each other*. As a dynamic and systematic dialogue between the two unfolds and develops, both theory and praxis are born. The effectiveness and influence of such theory will depend on the degree theoretical and experimental models are brought into creative interaction with each other.

A graphic schema may be helpful (see Figure 1). I wish to use the term "theory" in this book to describe the dialogical process which yields a systematic set of ideas. The partners in this theory-building process can be theoretical models on one hand, and experimental models on the other. We use broad, holistic theoretical models to describe the whole of reality in a parish, and more specific, particular experimental models to describe particular dimensions or aspects of the parish. In this dialogue educated guesses or conjectures (hypotheses) are developed which provide a kind of bridge between the theoretical and the practical. Intentional and deliberate change occurs when experimental models are developed out of theoretical models. New theory develops as theoretical models are born out of experimental models. Hypotheses invite these partners into dialogue, harmony, and creative tension with each other.

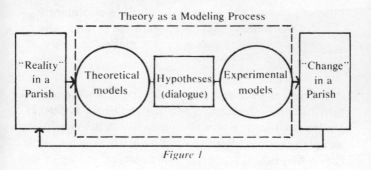

Theory as a Modeling Process

Figure 1

In modern society, and in our modern church, a tendency to discount the value of theory seems to be apparent, as if it were an "ivory tower exercise in irrelevancy." And yet common sense suggests its importance:

For one thing, you can ignore (theory). You can say that it is impractical . . ., too abstract and obtuse to be of much use in planning and operating day-to-day programs. The trouble with this choice is that it is unrealistic. The fact is that there are assumptions, concepts, and principles—theories—behind everything you do, whether you are conscious of them or not. . . . If you aren't clear about what your theory is—or even whether you have one—the chances are that you will end up with a hodgepodge. You will use different theories in different times or situations, or conflicting theories for different decisions in the same situation. You won't know why you are doing what you are doing. There is a cliche in the applied social sciences—often attributed to Kurt Lewin—that nothing is as practical as a good theory to enable you to make choices confidently and consistently, and to explain or defend why you are making the choices you make.[7]

Using the schema above as a framework, I would now like to outline how I will proceed (see Figure 2). Dulles' well-known models of the church provide for us an apt *theoretical* description of a parish. A star symbol (✭) is helpful for recognizing the integral nature of the five dimensions of church as delineated by Dulles.

Then I turn to the individuals who comprise a parish, and specifically to how they learn and grow. A circle divided into three sectors (⊕) suggests three unique yet complementary ways we grow throughout life:

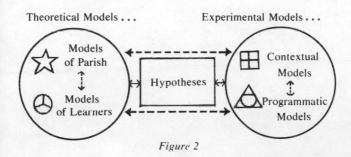

Figure 2

It becomes apparent that a satisfactory understanding of what it means to become church is difficult without an analysis of how I learn in the midst of a community.

The issue of the relationship of these ecclesial and educational models then leads to some educated guesses or hypotheses about the practical ramifications in a parish which seeks to become an ecclesial community of learners, or a learning community of worshipers.

I also develop two experimental models, one for improving the parish as the context for adult learning, and the other for designing programs in adult learning. While the former describes the growing and collegial parish as a necessary context for adult growth in that parish, the latter is based on an assumption that growing *adults* are necessary for a growing parish. A square divided in four quadrants (⊞) is the symbol I have selected to model the collegial parish, and a triangle within a circle (◬) for persons as learners in Christianity. The challenge throughout this study is simply:

"How do we proceed to help parish communities and the individuals in these communities grow 'in age and wisdom before God and man?'"

2
Theoretical Models of Parish

Fr. Avery Dulles, S.J., has developed the best known and most helpful system of theoretical models available to us in his recent *Models of the Church*.[8] In this "critical assessment of the church in all its aspects," Dulles plumbs the depths of ecclesiology in a clear, popular and forthright exposition.

Dulles' use of "model" is clearly theoretical rather than experimental, descriptive of ecclesiastical reality rather than prescriptive of specific implementation. His five models are not meant to be mutually exclusive alternatives for various local churches, but complementary dimensions of every local church. Thus it is not correct to say that this or that parish is or should be modeled after this or that model. All five describe the mystery of local church from various perspectives. For this reason, I prefer to describe these models graphically in the form of a star (see Figure 3). To describe a parish adequately is to do so from all five dimensions.

Institution and community are the two foundation points of the star on which the other three rest. For me they express the very core of our human condition; they express the primary need we have for personal relationship (community) and the elaboration of that reality in

Figure 3

organized structures (institution). The three upper points of the star represent the essential dimensions of the mission of local church.

To view the parish as *institution* is to see the viable structural components of parish life, especially the hierarchical structure with the priests and bishop responsible for the sanctification of the laity. Continuity with the past and future are highly valued, as are the structures and laws which serve to establish a clearcut system of procedures and discipline. Involvement in parish life vis-à-vis the institutional model emphasizes *role* involvement (i.e., as priest, director of religious education, principal, parish council member, lector, parent, etc.), more than involvement simply as persons.

While effective with large numbers of people, excessive institutionalism runs the threefold risk of clericalism, juridicalism and triumphalism. In clericalism an excessive degree of power and influence can be wielded by clergy who in virtue of their commitment and commission have a "sacred ruler position power" matched by no one else (or even everyone else). Likewise excessive reliance on laws and given structures can take the breath out of a parish (juridicalism). And when creed, code and cult become exclusive

("outside the church there is no salvation"), triumphalism has raised its proud and ugly head.

In creative tension with the institutional model is
community. Here the parish is seen as a "mystic com-
munion," a community of people united more interior-
ally and personally than exteriorally and juridically.
Rather than an officially organized institution, the
parish is a family, or a family of families united in grace
and spirit. "For just as the body is one and has many
members, and all the members of the body, though
many, are one body, so it is with Christ. For by one
Spirit we were all baptized into one body—Jews or
Greeks, slaves or free—all were made to drink of one
Spirit" (I Cor. 12:12-13).

"We are one in the spirit, we are one in the Lord" is
the community model theme song. Parishioners are
people of God and priests servants to the people. Membership is by relationship more than registration, and
"church happens" wherever people are gathered in belief, worship and mutual support. The importance of
roles and offices (e.g., director of religious education) is
diminished in lieu of unique personal presence and relationship among all members.

While effective with small groups of people where
immediacy and involvement are in vogue, the community model in excess risks secularism, personalism and
elitism. With an overemphasis on present existential
gatherings of people as the *raison d'être* for parish, the
danger of discontinuity with the living stream of tradition becomes apparent. Likewise, a self-centeredness
and "country club" atmosphere may develop where to
be parish implies turning inward and nurturing one another almost exclusively. Another danger is elitism

where "you're nobody" until or unless you have become a part of such and such a community, group or
movement.

Indeed the community model can respond to a
modern and acutely experienced need for friendship
and self-esteem among people searching for increased
identity in Christ and his people. The institution model
contributes to an equally deeply-felt need for a clear
sense of the community's history and mission. [9] And it
is to the question of mission that we turn now in Dulles'
three final models.

These are arranged on the three upper points of our
star (see Figure 3) as sacrament, herald and servant.
While the institution and community models describe
what the parish *is*, these upper three clarify what the
parish *does*, i.e., the mission of the church.[10]

The *sacrament* model *(koinonia)* describes the
parish as a congregation that exists in the very event
which it gathers to celebrate. That event is the worship
of God in word and sacrament, usually at Sunday Mass,
when parishioners unite in love and gather to profess
their faith by celebrating what Christ has done. Thus the
community itself becomes a sacrament, a visible sign of
an invisible reality. The last supper described in John's
Gospel (Chapters 13-18) best exemplifies this model in
Scripture.

To be a member is to be part of that sign, part of the
worshiping community, actually experiencing God's
loving forgiveness in the whole life of that community.
Worship here takes on a weeklong meaning—something I do in every breath during the week as an
extension and expression of Sunday liturgy. When the
community does gather on Sunday (or whenever) for

Eucharist, the rich symbolism and ritual of the sacred drama catches my life at its deepest roots and brings it into intimate relationship with the life, death and resurrection of Jesus Christ.

Ritualism and romanticism are two obvious dangers of a too exclusive *sacrament* model. If the worshiping community is constituted too strongly as institution, liturgy may be celebrated too mechanistically, too rigidly, formally and authoritatively. The Eucharist can become an action of the priest only, with parishioners present only to "hear Mass!" On the other hand, if the community emphasis is excessive, the worshiping community may take on the character of an organismic serendipity where to worship is only and exclusively getting highly involved emotionally. Both extremes are tragic and can remove worshipers from a personal and mature experience of the rich symbolism, ritual and myth which are at the "source and summit" of Christian life.

While the sacrament model views church as present in an actual and present event, the *herald* model (*kerygma*) considers her more in terms of hope and promise than actuality. Here the parish exists to proclaim the good news, the kingship of God is at hand. Parishioners are those who gather to hear the word of God, and having believed, go forth to proclaim it in word and deed. Enriched from Scripture with an exciting vision of the world, apostles of the word go forth as prophets to speak for God to the human condition. "Go therefore and make disciples of all nation, baptizing them in the name of the Father and of the Son and of the Holy Spirit, teaching them to observe all that I have commanded you; and lo, I am with you always, to the close of the age" (Mt. 28:18-20).

Overemphasis on the herald model courts danger also. A too intense institutional emphasis can result in a dogmatic proclamation which in application can actually become indoctrination. This seems especially evident to me in fundmentalistic evangelization where all the problems of the sinner can be solved by the preacher and the message. On the other hand, an excessive community emphasis on the herald model can lead to rampant verbalism where Christians gather to pour over the Scriptures without guidance, expertise or continuity.

Indeed the herald model has been quite foreign to the American Catholic until recent years. Our Protestant relatives, on the other hand, feel they have long enjoyed a more full and personal relationship to God's word than Catholics. Since the time of the Protestant Reformation 400 years ago when Protestant and Catholic communities became polarized, Protestants emphasized the herald and Catholics the sacrament model, each to the partial exclusion of the other. What is hopeful in this day of incipient ecumenism is the realization that each of our respective recent traditions brings a much needed roundedness to the other.

The fifth model, *servant* (*diakonia*) is most exposed to the outer world. The servant parish is a wounded healer in the world, intensely involved in the action of changing the world for the better. Here one is fully a Christian only when working for others and against oppression, violence, tyranny and discrimination. To live in the world as a Christian is to work for social justice. "For I was hungry and you gave me food, I was thirsty and you gave me drink, I was a stranger and you welcomed me, I was naked and you clothed me,

I was sick and you visited me, I was in prison and you came to me" (Mt. 25:35-37).

The theology of liberation emerging in the past decade from Latin America is an excellent example of this model. Leaders like Fr. Juan Luis Segundo respond to the human plight of people as the starting point for parish. After consulting with hundreds of lay people to identify critical problems frustrating freedom and responsibility in their lives, he has developed faith communities of response to these issues.[11]

The case for the servant model is to the point. Justice is a constitutive element of Christianity. Poor and oppressed people abound in every community and throughout spaceship earth, and to some degree every person is oppressed or victimized by unjust structures and forces. Sisters and brothers must begin working hand in hand to become conscious of such injustices and work actively and effectively to overcome such victimization. Liberation is the payoff, and the assured promise of the Gospels.[12]

This model obviously emphasizes the active initiative and responsibility of laity who are to become leaven in the world. The relevance of such a model cannot be questioned. Yet again there lurks the dangers of overemphasis. Politicism is one, the identification and integration with political movements in such completeness that institutional identity becomes political rather than ecclesial. Thus ethical and political practicalities may override the wisdom of tradition. Secularism is also possible, the identification of the church's mission with that of society so that "horizontal" human resources and causes cloud any which are "vertical" or divine.

The servant model is often taken to refer exclusively outward, viz., what the church must do in society. However, such societal reform obviously goes hand in hand with the internal reform of the church. Indeed significant influence of the church in society is impossible apart from consonant realization of justice within. To preach justice without practicing justice is hypocrisy. The servant model thus challenges the parish to manifest in its structures and life the very justice, peace, freedom and love it purports to develop outside of its community.

Richard McBrien's "agenda for reform," for instance, provides a list of internal issues for consideration: viz., the democratization of church structures, decentralization of power, intelligent planning and research, official accountability, election rather than selection of bishops, greater limits on papal and episcopal power, improved ecclesiastical court procedures, the liberation and ordination of women, renewal of religious communities, greater decision-making freedom for clergy, ecumenical relationships, and a bill of rights including:

> The right to freedom in the search for truth, without fear of administrative sanction.
> The right to freedom in expressing personal beliefs and opinions as they appear to the individual, including freedom of communication and publication.
> The rights of persons employed by, or engaged in the service of, the church to conditions of work consonant with human dignity as well as the right to professional practices comparable to those in the society at large.[13]

The question as to which ecclesial model is most important is not so germane as is the question of which are most absent in our understanding of parish. As we have seen, all the models are valid, all are necessary, all are to be harmonized to provide an adequate theology of parish. In the least evident models are the promise of greatest potential. If, for example, the servant model is least understood or appreciated, perhaps it will provide the most energy and vision for our future. If the institution model has been discarded, it too is potentially pregnant with new life. So is the case with the other models.

3
Theoretical
Models of Learners

Dulles' models give us "handles" on the mystery of parish. To discuss adult learning in the parish, however, we need models of people that describe how growth and learning take place. For this endeavor psychology provides the bulk of data. The importance of understanding models of learning is crucial, I feel, for any serious consideration of how lifelong learning and adult education occur in the parish:

The way we understand the nature of the person to be educated will determine to a large extent just how we conceive the nature of the educational process and how we go about practicing it. There are a number of ways in which one can view human personality and its capacity for experience. Any one of them that is commonly held, whether conscious or implicit, is likely to exert a strong influence on every activity devoted to human beings, including how we direct our educational plans and practices.[14]

Thanks primarily to the work of Malcolm Knowles, I will distinguish three very broad theoretical models which seem to significantly influence parish life and education: the mechanistic, the organismic, and the transcendent models of the human person.[15] Each one is a way of looking at the reality of a person, as through a set of lenses and filters so to speak. While observing the same reality, each model provides a whole different view of the matter, like looking at an automobile through sets of variously shaped glasses.

The most common model of person is the mechanistic model. The world from this perspective is a machine and exists within the limits of space and time, is therefore measurable and predictable, and susceptible to change by outside forces and agents. People living in this world are like empty slates until written upon or sculptured by their environment and personal history. Such shaping and change are achieved by the application of external forces repeatedly and with reinforcement.

This model would incline us to view ourselves and each other as *reactive* people who when affected by external stimulants and catalysts, will respond predictably. To help people, then, is primarily to do something to or for them, to provide from the outside, whether in terms of service, instruction, training, leadership or whatever. Helping people change and grow is a matter of attending to whatever external stimuli, forces or programs might best affect their habits of behavior for the better.

Wayne Rood suggests many of the educational implications of this and other views in his 1970 publication of *Understanding Christian Education* .[16] The symbol for the mechanistic model of teaching and learning is the lecture room and library. Such "transmitting of the essentials" implies a content centered curriculum where the goal is to acquire the facts of one's cultural heritage. The student receives, absorbs, assimilates, and is evaluated on what facts are retained in memory. Biblical and creedal content is shared primarily to confront the reality of separation from God and to restore a satisfactory relationship with him. This model appeals strongly to rationalistic type people who have need for objective reality and solid, simple, clear-cut truth. Also, much of the fundamentalistic Christian education which has become so popular in America, especially in the name of evangelization, exemplifies this model. The publication of a catechism would also suggest this view.

The second model views the world through an "organism lens," seeing reality as a process more than a product, a constant interaction of forces. From this viewpoint a person has an inner reservoir or bundle of energies. What is inside the personality (i.e., in the wellspring of one's unconscious) is more important than what is outside. While some theorists see inner energies in conflict with each other as the best explanation of the organism, others see it as a personality thirsting for wholeness, completeness and integration. In either case, such a model would suggest that people are "proactive agents" more than passive recipients, as potential reservoirs to be tapped and elicited more than respondents to environmental influences.

In education the symbol of this model is the conference room and the method is dialogue and sharing. The teacher or leader is skilled in group dynamics and seeks to develop a positive and supportive relationship with the students. Evidence of growth and maturing indicates success, whatever its specific direction. In religion an encounter with the person of Jesus is nurtured, within oneself and in relationship with others. Much of the process oriented religious education of recent years has been based on this model. The publication of discussion resources also typifies this organismic view.

The transcendent model suggests that the world is part of a totality which is beyond space and time. This is a spiritual world where there is room for realities beyond immediate human experience, realities which often can be described only symbolically and metaphorically. As regards personality, over twenty altered states of consciousness have been delineated in recent years including dreaming, rapture or ecstasy, daydreaming and meditation.[17] Psychic phenomena are often experienced in these states which point to the reality of a "third dimension" in personality, that of transcendent inner space. Such a model would indicate that people are in touch with forces and energies much beyond the limits of their own conscious or unconscious personalities.

In education the quiet room symbolizes this model. Here the learner is free to retreat, to take a special place within himself/herself and enter into relationship with inner experiences, energies and forces. Students learn by inner discovery and the teacher's role becomes one of supporting and guiding on this journey. The teacher is skilled in the dynamics and aware of the dangers encountered in the exploration of inner space. Success is marked by the presence of inner peace and the release of powerful energies from within.[18] In religion this model suggests the soul as the meeting place of God and human beings where one can get in touch with grace and gifts and life wholly other than the natural:

For by his power to know himself in the depths of his being he rises above the whole universe of mere objects. When he is drawn to think about his real self he turns to those deep recesses of his being where God who probes the heart awaits him, and where he himself decides his own destiny in the sight of God. So when he recognizes in himself a spiritual and immortal soul, he is not being led astray by false imaginings that are due to merely physical or social causes. On the contrary, he grasps what is profoundly true in this matter.[19]

The schema (see Figure 4) of basic personality models positions these three views of a human being in three equal sectors of a circle. In industrial psychology these are often referred to as X, Y, and Z, [20] and are often seen as mutually exclusive. Thus an X—type theory describes people as passive individuals without much interest or capacity for responsibility. They must be told and controlled by external forces. Theory Y argues that people are creative and want to take initiative and responsibility. Theory Z assumes people are "transcendent self-actualizers," spiritually instinctive, more holistic, responsive to beauty and altruism, and the like.[21] Leadership is therefore authoritative, collaborative and prophetic respectively for the three views. I find these caricatures too mutually exclusive for my purposes.

In presenting these models of personality, I wish to make a case for their *complementarity*. I suggest that an understanding of a human being which is limited to only one or two of these models is too narrow, and that education so limited is ill-suited to deal with the whole person. In fact, whenever or wherever a person is consistently treated only as a machine, or only as an organism, or only as a mystery, then he or she is possibly

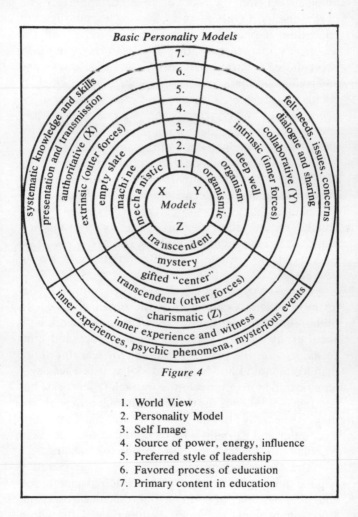

Figure 4

1. World View
2. Personality Model
3. Self Image
4. Source of power, energy, influence
5. Preferred style of leadership
6. Favored process of education
7. Primary content in education

being cut off from the roots of an important dimension of personality. In other words, lifelong learning or adult education implies a holistic understanding of the learner as *in some part* an empty slate responsive to presentation and transmission of systematic knowledge and skills; *in some part* a deep well from which is elicited wisdom by dialogue and sharing around felt needs, issues and concerns; and *in some part* a gifted soul open to transcendent inner experience and in awe and witness of the presence of mystery there.

While these three models are complementary, they are distinct. The mechanistic model (X) is by far the most prominent in modern culture, and will continue to be because it is the most effective for large numbers of people. Often called the preaching or transmission model, it is aptly demonstrated in the very successful Billy Graham Crusades we witness on television or in vast arenas.

I would hazard a guess that the predominent model for most religious educators is the organismic (Y). In training and experience educators frequently work with small groups where personal needs, issues and concerns provide the primary content for learning more than systematic knowledge and skills. It is a less systematic and more ambivalent approach to learners, but one rich in dividends for those to whom it is available. I think especially of the movements like Marriage Encounter and Cursillo which capitalize so effectively on collaborative dialogue and sharing for learning.

The transcendent model (Z) has engendered a popular movement toward transcendental meditation and other psychic phenomena in the secular world, and a consonant quest for inner meaning and gifts within religion. The Charismatic movement is the best example, and it is alive, well, impressive, effective and not a little threatening to adults limited to only X and Y perceptions of personality.

These models are meant to provide a theoretical base for interpreting lifelong learning. They are helpful in identifying world views and broad personality models for the purpose of clarifying underlying assumptions. Their greatest importance lies in providing philosophical and psychological categories to help us "check our glasses" about the reality we see, or think we see, in the local parish. It is now possible to suggest several hypotheses regarding lifelong learning in the local parish.

4
Some Conjectures About Parish and Learning

With the advantage of the above models of parish and learners, the development of healthy hypotheses or educated guesses is more possible. Theory is born of a dialogue between theoretical and experimental models. Theoretical models are the source of promising hypotheses to investigate and test. Experimental models are designs for action research whereby hypotheses are tested. A theory of lifelong learning in the local parish will articulate a system of ideas developed from this theoretical-experimental dialogue.

I am not convinced that sufficient research or modeling has been done with regard to the parish and lifelong learning to merit the proposal of systematic theory at this time. It is my hope that this work may stimulate such research and reflection. In any case I do consider it appropriate to suggest some significant conjectures derived from my own intuition, research and experience, not as guaranteed truths, but as a source of promising hypotheses to investigate and test. I will pose these (and the experimental models intimated by them) strongly and to the point, but I caution the reader to take them for what they are, only a few, limited, educated guesses suggestive of possible experimentation and research.

First, I am convinced of an integral relationship between the parish models and the personality models explored above. Parish life and mission and lifelong learning are inexorably intertwined. If a parish is growing toward a fuller realization of its wholeness as described in Dulles' models, members of that community can hardly escape growing to wholeness in their own lives. Likewise if individuals in a parish are engaged in lifelong learning, they will likely stimulate similar growth and development in their parish.

Lifelong learning in the parish is most frequently designed for large numbers, in a mechanistic mode with authorities and experts presenting and transmitting. Indeed some of this is necessary. But if lifelong learning is to become more collaborative with dialogue and sharing (organismic), and more transcendent with the sharing and witnessing of inner faith experiences, people will need to become part of much smaller parishes, or more likely, part of sub-communities in a parish. The trust and support necessary for an experience of organismic and transcendent learning are usually unavailable in large groups of over, let's say, thirty or forty individuals or families. Such small groups can be flexible and temporary, or more structured and continuous. They should be self-selecting and *not* established by geographical considerations alone.

I suggest a parish can have as many such sub-communities as there are members interested in joining; that membership in one or the other group should involve at least annual negotiation of written covenants or agreements describing each member's role, responsibilities and relationships in the group; that lay leaders be elected in each group who not only lead but also represent that extended family in a parish council; and that each group establish and nurture its own unique identity as one of several families in the parish. I believe an organismic and transcendent parish can develop best with lifelong learning happening formally in the midst of these communities. Parishioners not interested in such parish sub-communities or extended Christian families can still participate in the weekly parish-at-large celebrations which are in fact the usual manner of participation in parishes today.

Surely lifelong learning in the parish must involve adults in word, worship and service as well as members of a community and institution. Such involvement implies more active and responsible lay ministry where adults minister to one another in word and worship and caring service. How such ministry takes form is a matter unique to every parish and the sub-communities in it. But, at minimum, adults are engaged in a process of learning the story of Christ and the church in her tradition, especially as encountered in the present and including each individual's part in that story. The celebration of these stories in ritual and worship, in word and sacrament, is likewise a minimal requirement for lifelong learning. And having some part in bringing about the kingship of Christ in one's life and society is also necessary. Successful lifelong learning and parish communities demand these basic ingredients for maturing growth.

Again I stress the integral relationship of learning adults and growing parishes. As a parish takes responsibility for the individual growth of faith in its members, so the same members become capable of greater responsibility for the maturing parish community. There is an obvious and profound interdependency between the two, maturation in one affecting the other. Because of this, the models of parish have a mighty influence in lifelong learning, and the models of learning contribute much of importance to the parish. Thus I maintain that in any discussion of Christian learning the community in which that learning occurs is also to be considered.

This has been called the *contextual* dimension of lifelong learning.[22] The assumption is that for most of us, the parish is in fact the context for lifelong learning in Christianity. It is a kind of role model where much of what I learn about my relationship with God is the result of what I do in my parish community. The parish in its life and mission is a complex and sophisticated "classroom" or learning environment for adults.

> [We] must broaden the context of Christian education to include every aspect of our individual and corporate lives within an intentional, covenanting, pilgrim, radical, counter-cultural, tradition bearing faith community. A viable paradigm or model for religious education needs to focus upon the radical nature of a Christian community where the tradition is faithfully transmitted through ritual and life, where persons as actors—thinking, feeling, willing, corporate selves—are nurtured and converted to radical faith, and where they are prepared and motivated for individual and corporate action in society on behalf of God's coming community.[23]

In this dynamic learning environment called parish are needed specific and formal lifelong learning episodes which focus on some dimension of individual or corporate growth in faith. This is the *programmatic* dimension of lifelong learning. When conducted in context, such adult education programs become like dynamite which can quickly cut paths through mountains of ignorance or confusion.

Formal adult education programs can be made available to the parish at large; to special groups in the parish such as the pastoral team, parish council and other leaders; to various sub-communities in the parish as described above; to special interest groups such as parents or the divorced and separated; for individuals in quest of more intense learning; for specific events or functions in the parish such as retreats or liturgies; in response to critical problems that have emerged; in training for ministries such as visiting the sick, and so on.

Whatever programs are provided—consultations, seminars, debates, workshops, lectures, courses, training sessions, retreats or conferences, "packaged" programs such as Genesis II, exhibits, publications, films, meetings, etc.,—they are designed as the result of a dialogical need assessment process between leaders and learners. Leaders operating out of their expertise, vision and knowledge of both the parish community and adult religious education, and adults in touch with their felt needs and interests can put their heads together to respond educationally to individual and collective opportunities for growth with well designed and implemented programs.

In the following section I will discuss examples of *experimental* models for lifelong learning in the local parish, contextual—in parish life and mission, and programmatic—in specific learning episodes. It will become evident how these models depend on the above theoretical models of parish and learners for their vision and power.

5
The Parish as Context for Adult Learning

Dulles' models of church provide a good example of the kind of theoretical models we are able to use in advancing our appreciation and understanding of local parish. Other systems, models and theories are also available, of course. My utilization of Dulles' models in this work should not imply that they are the only or last word, only that at this time I find them the most lucid filters we have to interpret the mystery of local church.

With the assistance of such models we are able to develop our theory of parish. However we articulate our theory, I believe we must do so for ourselves in each parish. A systematic statement of ideas as to who we are and what we're about is the bedrock for what the parish will become. In many ways this description will be the prescription.

The implementation of such a dream is a matter for pastoral ministry. I see pastoral ministry as all that goes into a local parish as it becomes its vision and dream. It is the ministry of ecclesial wholeness in place and time. In pastoral ministry is integrated all of the life and mission of local church.

As the models indicate, pastoral ministry will bring a complementarity of ministries into tandem with each other, especially those "of proclaiming and teaching God's word, celebrating the sacred mysteries, and serving the people of the world."[24] Since the whole (pastoral ministry) is greater than its parts, its parts cannot be disintegrated into isolated and independent ventures. Unless worship, education and service become integrated and whole in the life and mission of parish, the community of faith will experience a painful schizophrenia.

I wish to elaborate because I observe serious problems in regard to the compartmentalization of pastoral ministry, especially in the proliferation of highly specialized and sophisticated ministries, and competition among them for power and ascendency. A simplistic solution, in caricature, is to reduce parishes to a size where a pastor can integrate most dimensions of pastoral ministry in his person, and build the faith community around him. While possibly attractive at first sight, this option must be rejected for many cultural, theological and practical reasons, not the least of which is any one priest's inability to incarnate the mystery of parish in his ministry alone. There may be exceptions where extremely gifted priests seem able to pull it all together, but as often as not, when they move on the parish pays the price, as lost sheep without a shepherd.

Another option is synergy, the "flowing together" of specialized ministries. With synergy in ministry, I believe, a parish can hope to become an integrated whole where the servant, herald, sacrament, community and institution models are reflected as balanced actuality. For me synergetic pastoral ministry includes:

1. the periodic development among leaders of a systematic set of ideas (a theory or theology) about the life and mission of the parish;

2. the integration of various ministries into a dynamic pastoral ministry which is much more than the sum of its parts;

3. the collaboration of all ministers in a pastoral team where power, authority and responsibility are shared, and communication open;

4. the effective overseeing of all pastoral ministry in the parish by a representative group of mature adults (elders), members commissioned by the community to lead and guide—a parish council.

These are the first and basic requirements, I believe, of any successful parish of the future. They are the necessary conditions for ministries of the word, worship, and service. And insofar as the parish is an educating and learning community, they establish the essential climate for adult growth in faith. Our theology of parish will scarcely allow any alternative to a well-rounded, consciously and deliberately integrated pastoral ministry shared by all who gather in the name of Jesus.

Because, as far as I can tell, some parish councils and pastoral teams are not doing so well, and because educational ministry to and by adults is conditioned on their adequacy, it may be helpful to share at least one experimental model which identifies some of the dynamics and challenges facing pastoral ministry.

Blake and Mouton have proposed a helpful model for this purpose.[25] In a grid format (see Figure 5) they have identified the two basic dynamics in any human community. Called the relationship and task dimensions, the grid describes a parish in terms of its life (relationship of members) and mission (the "job" members agree to accomplish). Each dimension is scaled from 1 to 9. The better a parish realizes its potential in either direction (life or mission), the higher a score along that continuum.

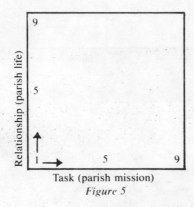

Task (parish mission)
Figure 5

Since parishes can be more or less committed to either or both dimensions, several kinds or types are evident with this grid model (see Figure 6). The "apathetic parish" is low on both community building and mission (1-1). Few interpersonal needs are met, few endeavors accomplished.

The "country club parish" gives high priority to developing healthy personal relationships and community, but little effort to accomplishing anything (1-9). To belong is to join a happy family of relative do-nothings. High value is placed on everybody being comfortable and appeased, and any feather-ruffling issues or tasks are squelched.

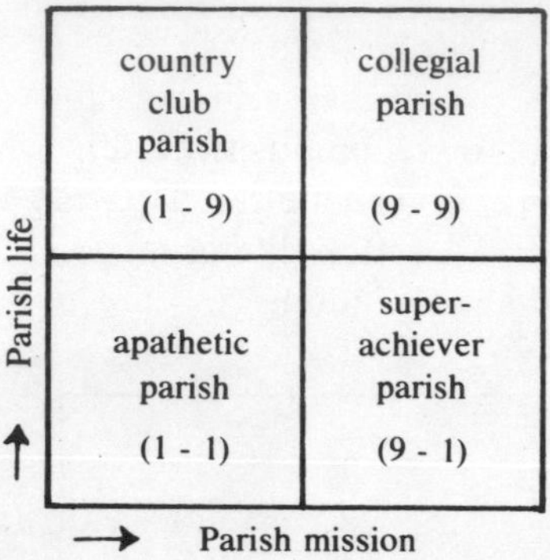

country club parish (1 - 9)	collegial parish (9 - 9)
apathetic parish (1 - 1)	super-achiever parish (9 - 1)

↑ Parish life

→ Parish mission

Figure 6

The "super-achiever parish" (9-1) shouts "damn the torpedoes, full steam ahead." Enterprises, programs, initiatives are developed with little concern for how people are affected by them. The leadership is authoritative and manipulative, but the job does get done.

The "collegial parish" (9 - 9) seeks strong relationships in community and a relevant and significant mission as well. Excellence in one dimension nurtures and supports congruent excellence in the other. In such a community people can expect to become part of an important mission much broader than themselves, and become much more themselves in that mission. Obviously again, education in the local parish depends on the kind of environment the parish provides. To the degree parishes can advance toward a collegial 9 - 9 style of parish, parishioners can learn what it is to be Christian in this integrated sense.

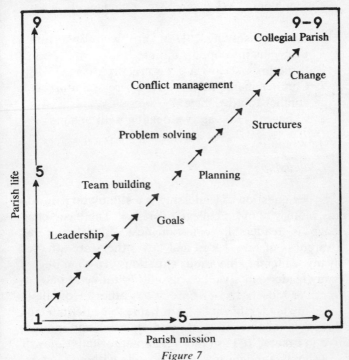

Figure 7

In my consulting with pastoral and parish councils, staffs and leaders, I suggest at least eight initial areas of concern apparent to me in the process of building collegial parishes (see Figure 7):

1. Leadership: "How are we leading?"
2. Goals: "Where are we going?"
3. Teambuilding: "How are we doing with each other?"

4. Planning: "What are we doing with each other?"

5. Problem solving: "How are we converting problems into opportunities?"

6. Structures: "How are we organized?"

7. Conflict management: "How are we utilizing conflict to advantage?"

8. Change: "How are we dealing with change?"

1. *Leadership*

The question of leadership is a stimulating start to any inquiry about a collegial parish.[26] The basic challenge is leadership consciousness—developing an awareness of how I lead and how others are affected by my leadership in various situations. To what degree is my leadership style heavily authoritative at one extreme or loosely laissez-faire at the other? How flexible is my leadership style? Am I able to be definite and directive in some situations and tentative and indirective in others? If I am too rigidly authoritative, few if any significant decisions will be made without the consent of the authority—me. While this situation may seem proper and attractive, the price is expensive in energy and time. The authority must be at every significant meeting, and any meeting where that person is not present is rather ineffective and wasteful. Priests, for example, who find themselves deluged with meetings can be the first to suffer the cost. "Can't the laity do anything without me?"

If an excessively laissez-faire leadership style is consistently and rigidly utilized, few decisions will be made apart from group deliberation. A parish council can easily become bogged down with a plethora of relatively insignificant "nuts and bolts" decisions which block and frustrate independent responsibility. Again, I fear, priests can pay the greatest price, having to come weekly and monthly to a confused and frustrated governing body incapable of making the many decisions that can and should be made independently. I hear of several bishops and pastors who have become so frustrated by the seeming inertia of pastoral and parish councils that they have discontinued them.

I suspect the pendulum-swing effect here. Before the catastrophic transitions occasioned by the second Vatican Council, parish leadership was primarily authoritative with the pastor ultimately and immediately responsible for almost all decision making in the parish. When the "people of God" movement toward greater lay involvement and responsibility occurred in the late sixties and seventies, the pendulum occasionally swung to an excessively laissez-faire extreme where important decisions were left to the whim and caprice of sometimes ill-informed and untrained (in the ways of church) lay people, however well intentioned and committed.

So that now it seems we are experiencing something in the way of anarchy, confusion and disorder in the church. Often there is evident lack of integrated leadership in parish life. Nevertheless, dedicated priests and people, burned and frustrated by their experiences of autocracy on one hand and anarchy on the other, are turning to a vision and practice of truly shared responsibility and collegiality. One key to such shared ministry is in my view a conscious and skilled use of power and authority through appropriate leadership styles.

In their superb *Management of Organizational Behavior: Utilizing Human Resources,*[27] Paul Hersey and Kenneth H. Blanchard suggest four simple styles of leadership—telling, selling, participating and delegating. Good leaders, the authors suggest, are able to use all four styles in varying kinds of situations. The *telling* style is appropriate with very immature groups of followers where there is limited experience and/or education, or where people are not able or willing to take initiative and responsibility, when they are passive and deferent in their behavior. These parish council members, however mature in other dimensions of life, perceive themselves as "rookies" or beginners in church governance, and naturally at first require a great deal of direction as well as socio-emotional support in their parish council dealings. The pastor or other leaders who expect them to immediately take significant responsibility or make enlightened decisions about the parish community are in for an experience of frustration that few can endure without bitterness or disillusionment. This dilemma is resolved only to the degree that the group matures in its understanding and ability to function in its appropriate role.

With more mature groups, or in more mature instances, the parish leader can move to a *selling* leadership style where participants become more actively involved in significant decision making, becoming more reactive than passive in behavior. Here a stronger relationship between leader and others is required to make decisions or accomplish tasks, a relationship that is not so critical for the "telling" style. A leader is "selling" a parish council when he or she suggests some significant change or project in the parish with a rationale for support. Others then *react* to the proposal with respect and dispatch with support or not, and then accept, alter or reject it in their deliberations and actions.

As the group becomes even more mature, a *participating* style becomes advantageous for the leader. Now while still giving a considerable degree of socioemotional support to the group or situation, she or he can now sit back, as it were, and participate as others begin taking increased initiative and responsibility. Now we have a parish council where leadership more and more shifts alternately from one person to another. Leaders participate as appropriate. The leader of this kind of group, a parish council president or pastor for instance, leads best when allowing the other members to "take their head."

A *delegating* leadership style is important when a leader is working with a very mature group or person quite capable of "picking up the ball and running with it." Here good leadership is evident in *diminished* relationship with followers and a *lessened* involvement with their tasks and responsibilities. A kind of healthy independency develops where those mature enough to accept significant delegation themselves become leaders in their own right without having to be dependent for personal support or direction from a leader, boss or superior.

Leadership obviously becomes problematic when a leader uses a "telling" style with a mature group or person, or a "delegating" style with the immature. Herein lies the leadership dilemma as I diagnose it in modern parishes. An autocratic leader frustrates a maturing community as a laissez-faire leader frustrates an immature community. A rigid "telling" style runs the risk not only of frustrating the energy and responsibility of the more mature, but also of reinforcing the naiveté and dependency of the very immature. I am not happy about parishes where only "telling" leadership is in evidence, or where parish councils have been abolished or not developed in the first place. Until or unless the potential leaders are given the opportunity to participate increasingly in leadership they will never learn how to do so. I am equally disenchanted with parishes where there is leadership by default, where all too much is delegated to people and groups quite incapable of dealing with the matter. The leader in the parish, whether pastor, professional or lay, does well 1) to be aware of the dominant or primary leadership style he or she usually uses, 2) to measure that dominant style against the relative maturity of the particular person or group in which one is leading, and 3) to be aware of opportunities to use personally less preferred styles in situations which call for them.

Needless to say, I am making an important assumption on what underlies this discussion of leadership styles as well as what is yet to follow. And that is that the monarchization of the church, which has been appropriate in past monarchial cultures, is simply not a satisfactory model in modern times. Democracy is better designed for modern times and people, and also has deep roots in the New Testament where the entire people of God are the church, a chosen race and royal priesthood (1 Pet. 2:9). The laity as church have every right and responsibility to be involved as leaders and significant decision makers in every parish.

Yet this is not meant to imply that pastors are not privy to a unique and special authority by their very office of shepherding. In virtue of ordination a pastor is commissioned officially to lead all the public activity in a parish community. If this leadership is thrust upon a community tyranically or autocratically, we can observe a monarchial and debilitating leadership ministry. On the other hand, if a pastor is deprived of or negligent in the use of some kind of overseeing veto power where, in rare and serious instances, he must "tellingly" force an agreement for the good of a community, he in fact is not empowered or enabled to function as pastor.

The challenge, it becomes clear, is how to guarantee and develop genuine participation in decision making (leadership) by the laity while preserving the office, function and leadership of the authorized shepherd. The dilemma is well broached, I am convinced, with a mutual understanding and skill by both clergy and laity in the use of one's dominant as well as alternative leadership styles.

2. *Goals*

"If we don't know where we are going, how will we know if or when we get there?" Leadership is impossible without vision. Collegial leadership requires collaborative vision. Developing such a community vision is the task of goal setting.

Each parish, as each individual, has its own

unique history and story, its community myth. This story reflects a community awareness about who it is, where it has been and where it is going. It is the story of this people as they fit into the long winding stream of Christian revelation. It is found in the heart and experience of the community and is expressed in its stories, architecture, customs and programs. A community's story is what gives it identity and purpose, and a continuity of past, present and future.

A collegial parish is aware of its story. Some can tell it. Others can point to it in a parish symbol or sing it in a parish song. To be in the community is to become part of that story, to draw from it and contribute to it from one's own identity. A self-conscious parish will naturally tell and act out its story, in season and out of season, like the home visiting of new members by the old when in many ways the story is told, in word and deed.

Some of the most successful parishes I know are those that have decided to understand their story and express it in some kind of symbol or logo which appears on banners and in communications for all to relate to and assimilate. This parish symbol is a graphic model expressing the community's self-identity. It is not easy to come by and seems to require extensive research, reflection, dialogue, study and artistic expertise. The importance of such an identity symbol is not missed by modern businesses and corporations which seek to develop and reflect a healthy, positive identity and image. They know the tremendous influence such public identities have in their life and mission, and of course their success and failure.

Goal setting happens effectively when a parish

identifies what it sees as its future identity. Setting goals is like developing an outline of the future chapters in a parish's story. If goals are conscious, articulated, written, symbolized and communicated, they can generate immense energy and power toward the unfolding of that story into history.[28]

There are many ways I have noticed goals being discerned, both informally and formally.[29] What seems of the utmost importance to me is that 1) these goals be developed out of the context of the parish's unique self-identity (and not simply taken on from somewhere else), 2) that they be reviewed, revised and proclaimed formally at least once a year as part of the parish ritual, and 3) that they be imaged and reflected in a community symbol which both integrates the past, present and future, and tells the whole story without words.

3. Team Building

Building a team raises the issue of collegiality in terms of how roles and relationships are discerned, defined and developed in a parish.[30] It implies that parish leaders are committed to shared ministry in pastoral teams of one kind or another. "Partners in ministry" is the theme that best expresses the assumption underlying team building. Once full-time, professional leaders in a parish concur in principle to become a team of partners, the process of ongoing team building can consciously and deliberately ensue. The temptation seems to be that parish leaders get so caught up in their specific tasks or ministries that they come to take for granted their collaboration and neglect team building. Attending to team building means establishing and maintaining trust, clarifying mutual expectations of each other, and working simultaneously and together on the many tasks necessary for the accomplishment of mutually desired goals.

I recall one of the best team building strategies I have ever experienced. I was a leader in a 900 family parish in Combined Locks, Wisconsin. Every Friday morning the pastor and I would meet to discuss a single agenda item: "What are your joys and sorrows about our mutual ministry this past week?" In the answering of that question with each other (not always a pleasant task for fear of hurting and being hurt), we grew into a highly energetic, effective and collaborative team.

We needed to deal with many questions about who had what leadership responsibilities and how they related with each other, what were our hopes and fears about each other and each other's ministries, what strengths and weaknesses each of us brought, and what assumptions (many of them false) we had about each other. Here we were able to share frustration and excitement, and occasionally even tears of joy and/or pain. In all of this, of course, an immense amount of trust was developed among us.

Since then I have been privileged to be part of several excellent teams, and in every case a mutual trust is the very foundation of success and satisfaction. If larger than five or six, it is extremely difficult in my experience to develop and maintain this degree of trust. To develop a team also takes time, more in the earlier stages of development, less later. Not only hours, but full days now and then are part of the investment team members must be willing to make. That time together—and alone—is necessary for a small group to develop its relationships and accomplish its work together. Needless to say, I believe pastoral teams should include only full time personnel, including pastor, associate pastor(s)—whether clergy, religious or lay—DRE, principal, liturgist, parish administrator or whoever lead on a full time basis.

Besides establishing trust, team members will need to continually clarify their mutual expectations of each other. Annually a clear, simple and written covenant, understanding, agreement or contract might be developed which specifies what is expected of each other, and especially of the leader in that pastoral team. These can be developed annually by asking each team member to list (preferably on large newsprint) "how I would like to function as part of this team" and then to place the lists side by side to negotiate agreements and differences. Some of the questions to ask may include:

How often will we meet, where, when, for how long?

Should our meetings begin and end on time, or should we be more flexible?

Who should be the chairperson; shall the job rotate?

How formal or informal would we like these meetings to be?

Who will keep records of our actions and decisions, how to file or distribute them (if at all); shall this job rotate?

How will the agenda be developed, when, and by whom? How changed?

How should we participate in these meetings, what norms or unwritten rules will guide our behavior?

How will we make our decisions, by the pastor, majority vote, consensus?

Will we pray, how and when?

How about absentees; how should they excuse themselves, and how should they "catch up"?

How are responsibilities to be accepted (appointed or negotiated)?

How should we go about solving problems we are having with each other?

How responsible are we to be to each other, how accountable?

How will we check, monitor and evaluate our progress?

Will we work primarily on our mutual tasks, our relationships, or both? How?

Should we encourage, tolerate or avoid conflict? Under what conditions?

Should we invite outside consultants to help us grow as a team? When? Who? Where?

How do we change these agreements?

Out of these kinds of questions a succinct understanding of who and what the team is about can emerge which will successfully clarify many faulty and foolish assumptions and expectations that pastoral team leaders and members may have of each other. The product of this kind of deliberation should be a succinct one or two page statement, agreement or covenant which briefly answers these and other similar questions. This agreement should be in the hands of each member and serve as a kind of constitution and bylaws for the group (although it does not have that kind of formality). I encourage these "pastoral team covenants" to be written, not to establish a static and straight-jacket relationship with each other, but to handle the problem of shifting expectations and unchecked assumptions. Over the course of a year persons on a pastoral team change, and often do not notice, or forget to tell others. Assuming that the others have changed their perceptions and decisions about the team in the same way, they alter the common understanding without negotiating the change, and the team is disrupted. A written agreement can be changed frequently, but only after being negotiated with all the members of the team. Again I recommend that such covenants be reviewed and renegotiated at least annually in most situations, and certainly whenever new people come on board.

An outside consultant knowledgeable and skilled in the theory and technology of team building can be an excellent catalyst for any team, and I strongly encourage every diocese to have available to parishes professional consultants (often called organization development [or O.D.] consultants) who can diagnose team problems, provide helpful resources and training opportunities, share appropriate instruments so that teams can find out about themselves,[31] and whatever else will facilitate the growth and development of pastoral teams.

4. *Planning*

Regardless of the time spent in building a successful team it will in all likelihood be for naught if
pastoral leaders and teams do not do adequate planning. Note that I suggest planning as the primary responsibility of the pastor and other full time, professional parish leaders, and not an enterprise to be extensively engaged in by parish councils and committees with relatively little information, experience, expertise, time and opportunity. The role of these groups
is to be consulted, to oversee, monitor and evaluate
the plans of the pastor and other professional and volunteer leaders, not to directly design them. I have not
yet found a parish council or committee capable of
collaboratively developing a comprehensive plan for
the parish. I have found many who, when presented
with the planning of its professional and volunteer
staff, have lent considerable wisdom with appropriate
questions, suggestions, criticisms and a wealth of
other contributions, not the least of which is enthusias-
tic support. And of course, when it is time for decisions to be made about alternative plans, it is the representative group of lay people who make those final
decisions in the best interests of the parish community
at large.

There are many ways to develop and communicate plans, and probably the best way in each parish is
the method most favored by the planners—the pastor,
pastoral team, professionals and/or volunteers. I will
suggest only one method here, simply because it is the
one I prefer. It is popularly called an MBO (management by objectives) approach, refined by W.J. Reddin[32]

into a three dimensional format.

The first dimension is developed by answering the question: "What are the effectiveness areas for which I am responsible?" Here the leader strives to identify those areas of activity where he or she expects to accomplish something. Probably there should be listed no less than 3 or 4 effectiveness areas and no more than 9 or 10. In essence these effectiveness areas are similar to the catagories of a job description except that they seek to describe "outputs" (accomplishments) rather than "inputs" (responsibilities). Off the top of my head, some effectiveness areas in a normal parish that may need to be addressed are:

preparation of parish communications
visitation of the sick
spiritual direction
liturgical celebration
quality of facilities
pastoral team administration
ecumenical liaison
diocesan communications
pastoral counseling
school administration
social action coordination
adult education direction
youth ministry development
elementary religious education
social activities promotion
classroom teaching consultation
family education development
liturgical ministries training
athletic programs coordination

musical leadership development
parish geo-social research
financial management
parish soccer league development
parish information coordination
Rite of Adult Initiation implementation
liturgical dance choreography
human rights advocacy
ongoing professional development
home visitation
bingo nurturance
death and dying ministry
plant maintenance
personal study/research
art coordination
Cursillo development
Marriage Encounter
pastoral planning
retreat coordination
youth retreat development
housing for the elderly
parish council effectiveness
board of education development
social action committee training
Jewish-Catholic dialogues
Catholic Family Movement
Genesis II implementation
sacramental preparation
neighborhood apostolate
prison ministries
prayer group organization
Charismatic movement leadership
board of education administration

parish personnel administration
parish membership development
special activities coordination
Right to Life promotion
children's liturgy quality
curriculum evaluation
guest homilies coordination
parish leadership training
migrant farmworkers activities
area/diocesan consultation
divorced/separated reconciliation
pre-cana programming
altar servers
church/sacristy furnishings
devotions coordination
volunteer teacher training

Already we note the dilemma of overextended pastors and leaders who try to become effective in too many of these areas simultaneously. Again I recommend that a pastor and each member of his pastoral team help one another make a list of effectiveness areas that need attention in the parish, and then each organize a list of 3 to 10 of these (or only 1 or 2 if a volunteer or part-time worker) for which one wishes to be responsible. Where there is duplication and overlapping, negotiation between members of the team will be necessary to clarify roles and relationships.

After identifying one's effectiveness areas, planning can then move quickly to the second dimension, viz., the setting of objectives. The question now is: "What do I want to accomplish in each of my effectiveness areas, and by when?" Here I want to list several specific accomplishments that I would like to see in each effectiveness area. In the "preparation of parish communications," for example, I might wish to list:

1. By each Thursday evening edit and produce the weekly bulletin.
2. Quarterly preparation of a pastoral letter to parishioners.
3. June preparation of annual report to parish council.
4. Minimum of four parish stories to diocesan paper.
5. Design and implement plan for "neighborhood caring communication system" in the parish.

The third dimension to this MBO approach is the design of the strategy for accomplishing the objectives to which I wish to give priority in order of time or importance. Included in this strategy is an estimate of how much time (in hours and/or percentages) I expect will be needed to accomplish the task, e.g.,

1. By each Thursday evening edit and produce the weekly bulletin.

Strategy (or plan)	Time estimate/ % of 40 hr. wk.
collect and arrange info items	½ hr.
draft a meaningful message	1 hr.
organize for secretary	½ hr.
proofread for inevitable mistakes	½ hr.
	2 ½ hrs.
	or 7% per week

In this example I have gotten very detailed to demonstrate as clearly as I can how a strategy and time estimate are developed. One can fall to the temptation of becoming overly precise and detailed which can prove to be counterproductive. On the other hand, it is helpful to have in hand a plan which includes: 1. 3-10 effectiveness areas; 2. several objectives for each area; 3. strategy and time estimate for each objective.

With this pastoral plan for each person many developments can take place:

1. I can see what I'm doing, where I'm going, how I'm getting there.
2. I can share and negotiate my plan with others on the team.
3. I can communicate and develop it further with my parish council.
4. I can monitor my own effectiveness, become more accountable to myself and others.
5. I can reduce over-commitment; make better use of time.
6. I can change it when and as appropriate, and know why.
7. I can plan more time for prayer, leisure and recreation.
8. I can delegate tasks and responsibilities more extensively and effectively.
9. I can learn what others are doing from their plans.
10. I can begin developing trends rather than working in the same circle.
11. I can explain to people what I really do for a living!

12. I can become more clear about my priorities and those of others.
13. I can observe and accept what I am not doing and should not be doing in my ministry, and rely more on others to do it if it should be done.
14. I can relax more.

If these plans are developed concisely by each member of the pastoral team, they can then be compared and integrated in such a way that unnecessary duplication is avoided on one hand, and all critical effectiveness areas are covered on the other. Moreover, members of the team can "bid" for the type of participation they would like in the effectiveness areas of others. Assuming that one person is *responsible (R)* for a specific activity, the others can "bid" or be invited to become *active agents (A)* in that project, or *consulted (C)* about significant decisions in regard to it, or simply *informed (I)* or in communication about the matter. Other categories of participation can be delineated and coded so that the role of each member of the team is described in relationship to each and every one of the team's activities. These can then be put into a simple matrix, as in Figure 8.

To take one item as an example, we see that in the case of "sacramental preparation," the DRE has chosen to be *responsible (R)* as leader, the associate wishes to be an *active agent (A)* or participant in that area, the principal and adult education director are to be *consulted (C)* on significant problem solving or decision making issues that arise, and the pastor wishes to be kept *informed (I)* . Roles and relationships are determined by team members according to what is

Effective areas or programs	Pastor	Associate	DRE	Principal	Adult Ed.	Etc.
1. preparation of cummunications	R	C	A	I	I	
2. school administration	A	I	C	R	I	
3. Cursillo development	A	R	I	I	A	
4. prayer group organization	I	A	C	I	R	
5. curriculum evaluation (school)	C	I	A	R	A	
6. home visitation	R	A	A	A	A	
7. social action coordination	I	R	I	I	A	
8. liturgical celebration	A	R	C	C	C	
9. quality of facilities	R	I	C	C	C	
10. musical leadership development	C	A	R	I	I	
11. ecumenical liaison	A	C	I	I	R	
12. sacramental preparation	I	A	R	C	C	

etc.   etc.   etc.

Code: R - Responsible for area or project as leader
A - Active in project as participant
C - Consulting in project as requested
I - Informed about project as appropriate

Figure 8

most appropriate to their respective offices, talents, and interests. While this may seem a laborious task, I have found that an immense amount of clarification ensues as to mutual roles and relationships. "Who is responsible for what?" and "What are the roles others wish to play in regard to that area?" are important questions that need answering in order for a team to function more effectively.

One other matter comes to mind. If a pastor has no team, he must obviously share many of these responsibilities with volunteer lay people. Where this is the case, usually in smaller parishes, the complexity of functions and roles is diminished considerably, and the planning and role clarification described above would not be necessary.

In any case, this kind of planning and role clarification is probably not an activity a parish council would engage in. These are executive and professional functions appropriate for a pastor and his team. This is the kind of information the team should present to the parish council for their advice and consent, review and evaluation. I am concerned about so many parish councils becoming too administrative and executive, actually taking upon themselves many, if not most, of the volunteer activities and responsibilities in a parish. Their meetings then become program planning and development sessions rather than deliberative, policy making, overseeing meetings. I would like to see them become more legislative, more overseeing, more reflective. I would liken the pastor (and his staff) to the president of the United States (and his staff), and the parish council to the Congress. The parish council represents the people of the parish in important decision making. the pastor and his staff are the administrative and executive body of lead agents in the parish. Where there is a serious conflict between the two, a rare exception in most parishes, the pastor, as the United States president, has veto power in order to force the agreement necessary to resolve an issue for the good of the whole community.

In my experience, a pastor and his team generate and draft, perhaps three-quarters of the significant issues, recommendations, policies, and decisions that need attention in a parish council setting. These are brought to the parish council for deliberation where appropriate legislation and decision-making takes place. I suspect many parish councils are meeting too frequently and with too little preparation to make significant deliberation possible. Much of that preparation is, in my estimation, the responsibility of the pastoral team.

The parish council and its committees are more legislators than executors. They should have some objectivity about all the activities that go on in the parish and not be a gathering of those who are actually doing all the programs. In the ideal order a voting member of the parish council should no more be responsible for a specific program in the parish than the DRE should be a voting member of the council. If these executive-legislative functions are not kept somewhat distinct, a great deal of confusion and frustration can develop around how the pastoral team should function in relation to the parish council and vice versa. Moreover, if in fact the pastoral team is doing the legislative work of the council, and the council members are doing the executive activities of the pastor and his team, each becomes overworked and overloaded in a function that is "out of phase" with its own.

5. *Problem Solving*

If problems are seen as opportunities for growth to be embraced and dealt with rather than stumbling blocks to be avoided in a parish, problem solving can become a very fruitful resource for the collegial parish. At pastoral team and parish council meetings, "We have a problem," should become a refrain to be met with hope and enthusiasm rather than despair and anger. The most effective pastoral teams and parish councils have a kind of "problem posing" attitude where consistently the search is on for the root problems that need attention. Good problem solving skills are helpful to developing this kind of attitude where we can comfortably "glory in our infirmities" because of the opportunities they may provide.[33]

Or to put it differently, problems, which are inevitable, can be diagnosed and dealt with actively and regularly, or left alone to simmer and erupt out of all proportion only to be treated reactively and defensively. Healthy and creative problem solving requires open communication, action research, and creative searching.

In a collegial parish where the communication system is open, everyone has access to all the information he or she needs to know. How many problems in the community result from incorrect or incomplete information running rampant!

Mature communication in the midst of problem

solving is also worthy of note. When there is a problem, energy is often running wild, emotions high. And communication—gentle articulation and active listening—becomes diminished. At times like this I have found it very helpful to check on what I think another is saying, by paraphrasing what I'm hearing to see if that is really what is meant. As often as not I find I am more than a few shades off. It is also helpful to become more conscious of giving credit wherever it is due in the midst of a problem. The tendency is to look so intently at the dark side of the matter or person that I miss the opportunity to give credit where credit is due. In the midst of problem solving, giving due credit generates the energy, creativity and support needed to arrive at the happiest and most fruitful solutions.

Action research is a simple method for finding solutions to problems, as well as the best problems for solution. Action research is a problem solving process which depends on the openness of communication among those solving the problem. It assumes that any problem solving group is capable of not only discerning important and crucial problems, but also of solving them without special experts or sophisticated knowledge.

Very simply, a pastoral team will define a problem needing attention and translate it into a possibility (a "how to . . . "). For example, "poor Sunday collections" may be the problem. The opportunity is "*how to* increase the Sunday collection." The "how to" has quickly moved us from a grumble (which cannot be solved) to a goal (which can be achieved).

Then the team shares all the available data relating to the problem. Notice they are *not* making decisions, not "jumping to conclusions" at this point. This is research, informal information gathering so that everybody working on the problem has the same relevant information that the others do. If any member is withholding information relating to the problem on the basis that it is not relevant (in his or her judgment) or that others should not be privy to that information, a "unilateral relevancy test" ("urt") has been made. And a team cannot long maintain trust and openness where this is frequently the case, nor can it solve the problem. This is often called the information sharing phase of the problem solving process and is characterized by a considerable amount of information sharing in a very nonjudgmental frame of mind.

Only after all the data is in and shared is a team ready to develop alternatives. Here again groups often jump to conclusions and make or take the first solution that appears. But in action research several alternative solutions are generated and each of them considered and weighed with an assessment of its relative advantages and disadvantages. When the group has in fact discovered two or three ways to "skin the cat" it is ready to choose one of them and work out a course of action.

What makes the problem solving process productive and fruitful is the degree of creative searching done in the midst of action research. In problem solving we have an opportunity to search for new, creative, never-before-conceived solutions to a problem. The right hemispheric functions of our brain are provided an opportunity to logically, imaginarily, effectively, dreamingly generate new possibilities. Conversely, in decision making we use the left hemispheric logical and rational functions to analyze and evaluate. Most problems in a parish are then dealt with decisively and critically before they have had a chance to be addressed uncritically. But until people can meet around a relevant problem creatively, by suspending for a time their judgmental functions so that new, imaginative, fresh solutions emerge, a problem cannot become a new opportunity for growth.

Participants at this creative search phase cannot take a judgmental, critical or decisive stance. The problem solving group agrees that for a time it will suspend its critical faculties and give leave to the imagination to run beyond the usual boundaries. Members also agree that each other's "crazy ideas" will be met positively rather than critically, that in response others will look for whatever germ or seed of a solutions is there. Usually I respond to your idea or contribution by reacting to what I don't agree with or like about it. If instead I would attend to what I most *like* about it, your creative energies would mount and expand. I can do this if I respond with three things I like about your idea, and only then what I wish could be developed in it. For example, if in response to our "how to increase parish income" problem you suggest the idea that every dog owner in the parish should bring his or her dog to church next Sunday, my ordinary reaction is to criticize the foolishness and irrelevance of your idea. But if I try hard to express three things I like about it, I might point out that 1) it might be a symbol indicating how our parish financially is going to the dogs; 2) many more people than usual might become more involved in solving the problem; and 3) it may provide something in the way of free fertilizer for the grass thus

reducing the grounds maintenance a bit. And indeed
the seeds of good ideas and solutions become evident,
because however the problem is solved, there might
well be a symbolic action, a greater number of people
involved, and a reduction somehow in existing expend-
itures.

The example is overdrawn and silly, to be sure,
but only to emphasize the point that many of the more
superb solutions to seemingly insoluable problems
come from overdrawn, silly, and imaginative ideas.
When a team allows itself to address serious problems
with a bit of this kind of "fantasy brainstorming," new
avenues and directions and reservoires can break
open, and problems soon prove themselves to become
opportunities for significant growth.

I have described these skills somewhat precisely
so that the contribution that problems can make to a
parish might better be appreciated. In delineating them
so, I risk giving the impression that they are sophisticated, difficult and rarely evident. Yet I find that good
leaders and team members already have and use these
skills, each in his or her own unique style. And they
are regularly used at pastoral team meetings where
every participant is clear about *when* we as a group are
sharing information (using the sensate and data gathering functions of personality), *when* we are generating
creative alternatives (using the intuitive and creative
functions), and *when* we are making very human and
rational decisions (using the feeling and thinking functions of our personalities). (Robert's *Rules of Order*
seeks to structure a format and procedure where these
processes can happen in even larger deliberative
bodies.) If a pastoral team or parish council is perform-

ing the same function at the same time, they are working in phase as a team, and the solutions to problems may become surprisingly clear and one's participation in solving them much more fulfilling.

6. *Structures*

Parish structures can be repressive or freeing. They are repressive when they become inoperative, inefficient or irrelevant. They are freeing when they integrate, stimulate and effect healthy change. In the parish the structures—organization, procedures and functions—need to be addressed and analyzed periodically.[34]

How are we organized? Where do our committees and groups interrelate and conflict? Where are we in competition rather than collaboration? How do we communicate and cooperate? What are our procedures for handling problems and conflict? A parish that faces these dilemmas pro-actively rather than reactively may well avoid the expenditure of much energy, time and psychic blood in foolish rivalry and ineffectiveness.

Many of these issues are mentioned elsewhere in this chapter, and are dealt with more extensively in the bibliographical resources mentioned. All of them contribute to the cleaning up of our systems in a parish, from developing covenants and plans to improving communications and leadership skills. But perhaps nothing brings the question of structures to a head than an organizational chart or grid.

Currently in our diocese a reorganization process

has been in vogue. In the course of this project over eight charts of how the department of education should be organized were contrived. Since the reorganization was meant to be widely consultative, many marched to the fore with chart in hand. Finally the bishop wisely took the matter in hand, and in the interest of the community as a whole announced his decision as to how the organization would look.

My inclination is that in most parishes the pastor and his team should be the primary agents in the development of organizational structure alternatives, of course with as much consultation as possible. I believe the parish council should be the body charged with the responsibility of weighing, deliberating, changing if necessary, choosing and approving the structures out of which the parish will operate. And I believe that the parishes which directly address the structural issues "in black on white" are most prone to enjoy both healthy and fulfilling relationships as well as effective and efficient ministries.

At the core of the structural issue is "Who is responsible to whom and for what?" Developing a schema of these interrelationships is, of course, a matter of modeling. An organizational chart is a graphic model of how people are organized, and a very helpful contribution to a pastor, pastoral team, parish council (and its committees), as well as and perhaps especially to the many volunteers who become actively involved in some kind of ministry as part of their membership in the parish community. It tells who are the leaders, with whom to communicate, who "owns" or is primarily responsible for solving problem-possibilities, what procedures are appropriate and so on.

I encourage any group that wishes to get itself effectively organized in the parish to develop a simple organizational model for themselves. While in fact the way the organization and relationships *really* work will not be as simple and clear-cut as described in such a chart, the schema will provide a healthy frame of reference and something in the way of boundaries or parameters within which people can more comfortably operate. They can also provide a helpful reference point for members of the pastoral team and parish to negotiate differences and solve problems.

Let these charts be ever so simple and concise! They need to include only the *key* roles and relationships, not all of them. The usual rule of thumb is the smaller and simpler the better. A chart with arrows and lines going every which way is good for generating humorous observations, but not particularly helpful for clarification.

The organization and functioning of parish councils is a matter that I wish to leave for another discussion except for an encouragement to have as few committees as possible, to have more of them organized on an ad hoc basis to accomplish some matter in a definite period of time, to allow the parish council to function as little as possible as a committee of the whole doing business that should be done in smaller committees, to have time at regular parish council meetings for ad hoc committees to deal with a matter on its own, and as I pointed out earlier, to assure that parish council members are not in fact functioning as program planners, executors or implementors at the meeting lest their very commitment and involvement to a program diminish their objectivity and responsibility for overseeing the whole of parish life and mission.

But I would like to share some thoughts about how the pastoral team might develop its organizational chart. Four types seem to stand out as common alternatives among pastoral teams, and I describe them popularly as the autocratic or boss model, collaborator model, synergetic model, and independent or laizze-faire model. They obviously range on a continuum from the autocratic to the anarchaic, from very "top-heavy" leadership to non-leadership.

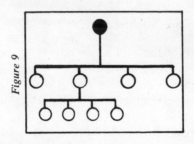

Figure 9

The autocratic model (see Figure 9) is the most frequently seen and describes a superior in relationship to his or her inferiors. Responsibility is owned by the boss who delegates whatever power he wishes to others, without losing control of course. While this model is appropriate for pastoral teams where team members are rather immature or on board for only a short time, it can also indicate an immature leader who lacks the self-confidence and trust of others to allow them a greater share in the pastoral ministry.

The collaborator model (see Figure 10) is a decentralization model where the leader seeks to share what is usually considered his responsibility and authority with a broader spectrum of associates. Here the leader strives to become more an equal among equals than a superior among inferiors. Whereas a parish priest who is not a pastor is often considered an "assistant" to the pastor in the boss model, here he becomes more of an "associate" pastor, sharing in the authority of the pastor to a greater degree. And so likewise with other members of the pastoral team.

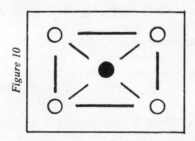

The synergetic model (see Figure 11) moves beyond shared responsibility to co-responsibility. On a pastoral team using this model, no longer is the pastor seen as unilaterally responsible for pastoral ministry sharing it as appropriately as possible. Rather the entire team is responsible as "co-pastors," and the authority is clearly with the team. The team leader, usually a pastor, is fully an equal among equals, a part of what is frequently called a "synergetic team" where as a result of this co-responsibility, individual gifts and energies flow together into a whole with more authority and responsibility than the sum of its parts or members.

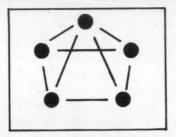

Figure 11

The independent model (see Figure 12) moves out of co-responsibility into independency. Here each member of the pastoral team does his or her thing after having clarified something in the way of what is each person's turf. It is really a non-responsibility model as far as teamwork is concerned, and while it may not get in the way of the individual progress of any member of that group, it negates the possibility of any kind of cooperative, collaborative or synergetic ministry.

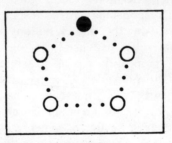

Figure 12

The ideal may seem to be the synergetic team model where co-responsibility is the norm. Yet I find this model opportune for only a very few of the most mature parishes in the country. I say that because while in our parishes we are moving from autocracy to decentralization (with what may be a temporary detour to anarchy and leaderlessness as observed earlier), I am not confident that given our tradition, history and ecclesiastical culture, to say nothing about our current theology of ministry or canon law, we can ask pastors to risk abrogating their official authority and responsibility to others less equipped to take it on. In fact it may likely be irresponsible to do so, except in rare parishes well out ahead of the rest of us in ability and maturity to deal with all the implications of pastoral synergy.

My hope is that as modern parishes mature, shared responsibility may become more and more co-responsibility, implying that other members of the parish and certainly the pastoral team are equally as well versed and trained as priests are today in the sacred and secular sciences as they apply to parish life. While I am convinced that this is where the church is going out of necessity as well as opportunity, I suspect that rarely at this time is the synergetic model possible except among teams of very highly and equally qualified members.

I have said very little about the boss model with all of the responsibility owned by the pastor because it is so common, so unfortunate, and so inadequate.

7. *Conflict Management*

Conflict is another matter that cannot be successfully ignored or suppressed. If it is, boredom results and lifelessness is rampant. The hallmark of a collegial parish is creative and constructive conflict. Conflict is often misunderstood to imply that between two antagonistic forces, people or groups, one wins and the other loses. The implication is that antagonism is necessary, and one party is right and the other wrong. Of course we know that rarely in any conflict is one person or group wholly wise and the other foolish. Both have some hold on truth, and both are in some part blinded. A collegial parish is one where there are frequent opportunities, effective procedures and expressed willingness to identify and solicit differences, to capitalize on them in a search for wisdom, and to do so in a spirit of trust, mutual support and healthy confrontation.

It has been observed that conflict is a function of caring. This would not be true if conflict is taken to mean aggressive hostility directed toward another individual or group. No one really needs this, or appreciates it. And little in the way of healing seems to come from it.

But conflict seen as entering into communication where my needs or interests are addressed without attacking another is a different matter. Such an attack usually comes out of an assumption that the other person or group "owns" or is responsible for my problem or conflict. In addressing the problem, I naturally address its owners—as *I* perceive the situation. The designated owners become defensive, and hostilities emerge.

For example, in the case of what I perceive as poor liturgy in the parish, it is very simple to "project" the anxiety I feel toward an exposed target, the pastor or director of music or whomever, and lay the blame for the entire problem on him or her. Should I muster enough gusto to actually confront the issue, I usually wind up confronting the person who I think is most responsible for it, who most owns it. "Father, your sermons are really inadequate." And on the surface, that *is* the problem as I perceive it.

The reaction of the pastor is usually not pleasant either. If he understands the projection (and he receives many in his ministry), he may be able to not only accept the condemnation but actually capitalize on it to further develop a relationship with me. He may even become aware that in fact he does own something of the problem, that he might need to become more responsible for his sermons. Sometimes, however, his reaction will be avoidance or hostility.

What happens among individuals also happens among groups in a parish, where one committee or organization is experiencing pain and projects the problem and its ownership on another. And so it is the liturgy committee or the education committee that is the cause for this or that problem.

Conflict management is the systematic bringing together of factions. A collegial parish requires an attitude, first of all, that accepts and encourages healthy conflict. There is some evidence to show that where this is so, the parish is both more stable and more creative. This attitude is best taught by those who are leaders in the parish modeling it in their behavior. If a pastor encourages creative conflict by asking for it, scheduling it, participating in it, a norm will become evident to the effect that "to care is to confront," supportively, positively, constructively. And because of it the community will be built up greatly.

Much work and experimentation has already been done in the matter of how to systematically and procedurally make the most of conflict in a parish context.[35] The primary axis of the entire process seems to be helping conflicting parties and groups successfully identify the problem, uncover their ownership of it (i.e., share of responsibility for it), and together plan the strategy for its solution. The result is that the problem gets solved, the parties become closer to each other in the process, and new energies unfold that would have remained dormant if the conflict had not been addressed. All this to say that healthy, collegial parishes seem to be those which not only accept but encourage conflict, provide healthy and mature procedures and opportunities to be handled, and are ever ready to capitalize on the high energies that resolved conflicts generate in building up the community.

8. *Change*

Change is an eighth area of concern to the collegial oriented parish. Some parishes, it seems, have decided to remain rather static. As Knowles observes, there is emphasis on conserving resources and a tendency to self-sufficiency.[36] The parish is closed to outside stimulants and resources ("we don't want the diocese in here!"), little risk-taking is evident, few mistakes are made or failures experienced. Decisions are final, irrevocable, made by legal mechanisms, and of course by those at the top.

The static parish is meant to be a smooth machine. In fact it is a closed system. Communication is restricted, flows one way, downward, and feelings are usually ignored, repressed or hidden. The building up of this community, as well as adult growth and learning in this environment, is well nigh impossible, of course, for obvious reasons.

Many parishes have caught the meaning of *metanoia*, or change of heart, and have consciously decided to be innovative, a growing organism. As I have noted, this implies that significant decisions are made as much as possible by all who are affected by them and usually in a problem solving methodology or mode. Such decisions are more tentative, and open to change where new data or situations indicate. More ambiguity is evident, and a higher tolerance for it necessary. Emphasis is on releasing the energy of people, and power is used catalytically and supportively. Risks are taken, failures experienced, and the attitude toward errors positive rather than punitive. They are opportunities for learning. This parish system is open, with an open flow of information up, down and sideways, with everybody involved having easy access to information. Feelings are expressed, accepted and dealt with openly.

The question of whether a parish wishes to be or become static or innovative is a very serious and important one. A commitment to the static, however covert, will of course frustrate all but sporadic out-of-community adult growth. If an innovative parish community is desired, immense energy in members can be released and focused on both personal and parish growth. Regularly and rather insistently, I feel, each parish—especially the leadership in that parish—needs to come up against that question: To what degree do we value the very concept of community growth and *metanoia*? To what degree are we committed to the relative comfort of sameness?

The choice about change is not confined only to whether or not to change, but also how a community proceeds in change. The change-style in some parishes is very controlled, systematic and measured. In others change is more random, spontaneous and free-spirited. It is obvious that both extremes are undesirable. But what does lie in the middle?

Malcolm Knowles observes a very helpful distinction made in the physical sciences between the models used by Newton and Einstein to explain energy and change in matter.[37] Newtonian physics, as I un-

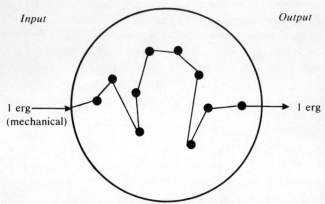

Figure 5-1. The Newtonian energy system

Figure 13

derstand it, sees change as a transforming process (see Figure 13). Introduce one unit of energy (an erg) into a system and it can be transformed again and again into another kind of energy. For every energy unit introduced, a different energy unit can be produced.

Einsteinian physics, on the other hand, sees change as a radiating process (see Figure 14). A unit of energy introduced into this system causes a catalytic, radiating series of reactions resulting in a large number of energy outputs.

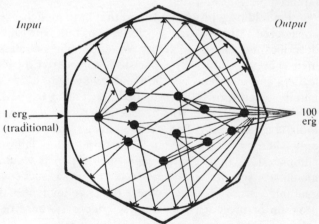

Figure 5-2. The Einsteinian energy system

Figure 14

The distinction has much to contribute, I suggest, to how a parish understands and utilizes change. If change is seen in a Newtonian context, every action will result in its opposite reaction. From a dollar I put in the collection basket, I can expect a dollar's worth from it. From every hour I give to changing and building up the community, I can expect an hour's worth of success. This is because I see change as the transforming of one kind of energy to another.

Using Einstein's model, change is better viewed as energy radiated than energy transformed. My dollar or my hour is considered more a catalyst which unleases many latent energies elsewhere in the parish producing the value of a hundred or a million dollars of hours in output. Since this is the case, in expending any given dollar or hour, I can expect to produce a hundredfold and more.

I'm told by a physicist friend that both models are considered valid in modern science, but that Newton's describes low energy systems while Einstein's models high energy systems. If a parish is considered by its leaders and members as a low energy system, a community where not much can be expected to happen, then its change-style will be one where most everything is tightly controlled, where changes are initiated only when the results are guaranteed and risk of failure eliminated. A high energy view of the parish would manifest itself in a change-style where a success-guarantee is not required, where the development of a program or project is not closely guarded, where results are not easily or necessarily measured.

In the extreme both seem unfortunate, a low energy view for restraining change to the limitations of its control, a high energy view for unleashing energies which can explode out of control. My bias, however, is to err toward the high energy side if necessary rather than the other, to see change in the parish in reference to the parable of the talents:

"Sir, I had heard you were a hard man, reaping where you have not sown and gathering where you have not scattered; so I was afraid, and I went off and hid your talent in the ground. Here it is; it was yours, you have it back." But his master answered him, "You wicked and lazy servant! So you knew that I reap where I have not sown and gather where I have not scattered? Well then, you should have deposited my money with the bankers, and on my return I would have recovered my capital with interest. . . . To everyone who has, will be given more, and he will have more than enough; but from the man who has not, even what he has will be taken away" (Mt. 25: 24-29).

In summary, then, the above eight areas provide examples of what can be done practically to better develop a collegial parish. I believe these are some of the most fruitful steps that can be taken to practically implement a theology of church in a particular parish. The Blake-Mouton grid directs us to the tension between the life of a parish (as community and institution) and its mission (as herald, sacrament, servant). It invites us to "tinker" with various models in a parish. The grid suggests several experimental models of parish (apathetic, country club, superachiever, collegial) and emphasizes the value of the collegial. The eight strategies or "interventions" describe specific actions which can facilitate growth toward collegiality.

Much of this comes by way of the behavioral sciences. While the behavioral sciences try to make the best of the human condition in the areas of personal growth, group dynamics and organization development, these interventions are helpful (and I believe crucial) only to the degree that they nurture the building up of personal faith and faith community. A misunderstanding of or blindness to what "putting on the Lord Jesus Christ" means and involves risks putting faith at the service of strategy, religion at the service of science, the divine at the service of the human. That will not do. Tampering with the mystery, dynamism and complexity of parish life, especially since it is such an important role model for adult growth in the parish, is downright dangerous without adequate theological background and understanding.

A solid liturgical background and interest are needed by the pastoral team engaged in the development of collegiality. Collegiality implies mature liturgy since liturgy and the liturgical year are the backbone of parish life. To be Christian is to live and celebrate liturgically. The new rite of Christian initiation is an important case in point. The rite suggests not only an effective organizational model for parish, but also many possibilities and parameters for planning parish life. To see the new rite as a "little something extra or new," or to assume that its implementation is limited to official liturgical rites affecting only those being baptized is to miss the point. Christian initiation is a model for the entire life and mission of a parish and the adults in it. The initiation rites presume that the entire community will be involved with candidates and catechumens in their journey to the mysteries of salvation. Evangelization, the invitation into Christian community, must come from a group of Christians witnessing to the value of Christianity in their lives and parish.

Especially during Lent when the catechumen begins a period of intense preparation, the community is needed to accompany and sustain these "elect" and each other.

The collegial parish also implies a relevant and effective ministry to the sick and oppressed, within and without the parish. For me this suggests that the pastoral team is actively identifying the critical problems in church and society which cry out for attention and response, and developing imaginative initiatives toward their solution. I believe that the inspiring success of what has come to be called theology of liberation or the liberation movement is precisely due to the accent of relevance evident in a local church community which claims responsibility for dealing with its blindness and paralysis. In these communities, of course, worship and learning are fully integrated with a personal and communal quest for freedom.

Finally, it is evident that adult learning must be or become an integral part of pastoral ministry in a collegial parish. In fact liturgical and service ministries require adult learning for their success. Moreover, we Christians have much to learn about ourselves and our faith journeys within the living stream of revelation and tradition. Much of this learning must be done in the context of parish life and mission:

> . . . like other pastoral activities, catechetical ministry must be understood in relation to Jesus' threefold mission. It is a form of the ministry of the word, which proclaims and teaches. It leads to and flows from the ministry of worship, which sanctifies through prayer and sacrament. It sup-

ports the ministry of service, which is linked to efforts to achieve social justice and has traditionally been expressed in spiritual and corporal works of mercy.[38]

I am inclined to see liturgical ministry as specialized in how individuals and community better worship God, educational ministry in how we better know God, the ministry of service in how we better serve God. Worship demands background and skills in the history of culture and liturgy, the use of sign, symbol, ritual, myth, the role of art and architecture and much more. Learning demands expertise in teaching, psychological development, group dynamics, use of space, and whatever contributes to heightened intelligence (including both reason and emotion, as Gabriel Moran emphasized)[39] not the least of which is an understanding and appreciation of the content of revelation and tradition. The ministry of service demands ability to discern real problems rather than pseudo-issues and to invite people and systems to move toward their solutions effectively and efficiently.

God forbid that a parish fosters three or more distinct and separate programs where the priest, liturgist, or liturgy committee "takes care of" worship, the educator or education committee learning, and the "missionary" or service committee the world! If educators and missionaries do not participate in worship, if liturgists and missionaries do not participate in learning, if liturgists and educators do not participate in bringing about the Kingdom of God in deed, we have a compartmentalized model of pastoral ministry. All must gather to deliberate and plan a synergetic pastoral ministry where the worshiping, learning and servicing concerns and expertise come to bear *together* on the faith life of individuals and parish life of the community they comprise. There are not three sets of programs pulling people every which way, but one integrated thrust which shouts forth in fact that "we are one in the spirit, one in the Lord."

My contention, in summary, is that adult education in the local parish is effected strongly by the kind of community that parish is becoming, what people experience there in their unique faith journeys. A serious pastoral responsibility is consequently to help facilitate that community as learner. Needed is knowledge and skill in the dynamics of community learning, enlightened by the wisdom of theological understanding, celebrated in parish life and liturgy, energized in freedom for all. Under these conditions we can attend to formal adult education, the planning and execution of specific learning events which are needed to assist maturing adults in becoming more whole in the context of the Christian community. We turn now to that challenge.

6
Programming for Adult Learning

The most popular way adult religious education is described in ecclesiastical documents is by the term "catechesis," whose purpose is to make a person's faith "become living, conscious and active through the light of instruction." While this description smacks of a mechanistic approach, it is frequently interpreted among educators to mean "echoing" (catechesis) and "standing within" (instruction) the living tradition of faith. In popular circles the term usually connotes transmitting a catechism of doctrine in some way.

If the theoretical models of learning described above are taken seriously, we are challenged with much more in adult learning than presenting a compendium or catechism of Scripture, doctrine and theology. While these provide the richest of resources for adult learning, I believe the primary task should be seen as a person's own discovery of his or her personal and spiritual identity in the context of Christian revelation. Consonant with this self-discovery is a liberation from all sorts of victimization—from blindness, ignorance, passivity—as one becomes more creative and responsible in the midst of life. "If you continue in my word, you are truly my disciples, and you will know the truth, and the truth will make you free" (Jn. 8:31).

"Am I not free? Am I not an apostle?" (I Cor. 9:1).

Loretta Girzaitis in her *Church as a Reflecting Community* provides an excellent summary of the task before us in programmatic lifelong learning:

1. to aid individuals to discover and to develop their potential as persons created according to the image of God;
2. to recognize the meaning of life and to respect it in all of its dimensions;
3. to incorporate the message of Jesus into one's personal life;
4. to articulate and to share the teachings of Jesus with others;
5. to understand and reflect upon the "signs of the times" so as to give direction to change in order to shape the future;
6. to provide opportunities for ongoing learning at all periods of adult life;
7. to participate in and celebrate life in the church, the community of believers;
8. to aid committed Christians to serve the needy, the poor, the lonely, the outcast, the discriminated against, and the segregated.[40]

In these goals is a strong emphasis on what individuals as learners must do for themselves: Discover and develop their own potential, recognize and respect life, incorporate the message of Christ, articulate and share the teachings of Jesus with others, etc. Parish adult education programming is to stimulate, aid, nurture such learning, not provide it whole and entire for incapable and unlearned respondents.

I wish to expand this concept by proposing an experimental model for adult learning which is depicted graphically by a circle within a triangle (see Figure 15).

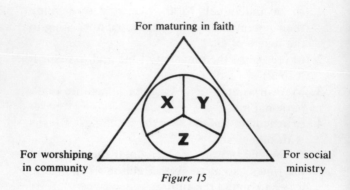

Figure 15

The circle represents an integrated model of learners, and suggests that adequate learning includes mechanistic, organismic and transcendent educational experience. This means that a learner can indeed be presented with systematic knowledge and skills by authorities and experts, but also that a learner explores felt needs, issues and concerns in dialogue and sharing, and enters within to touch and be touched by the presence and gifts of the Lord. "Behold, I stand at the door and knock; if any one hears my voice and opens the door, I will come in to him and eat with him, and he with me" (Rev. 3:20).

Such a holistic model of learning implies that adults are responsible for their own learning. Figuratively speaking, as one moves from X to Y and Z, he or she leaves the large lecture hall, moves to the small conference room and winds up in the quiet room. True, in each place one can choose to respond reactively or pro-actively.[41] But while it is often easy to remain reactive in the lecture hall, waiting while others take responsibility for my learning, this attitude is more difficult around the conference table or amidst the sounds of silence when alone. As one becomes more intimately involved with others and self, a noticeable shift in motivation and responsibility from dependency to interdependency occurs. One becomes more involved, more interested, more decisional, more responsible in learning.

While the circle speaks to the process of learning (i.e., how adults learn), the triangle depicts a thematic frame of reference for adult education programming. The three points of the triangle specify the most important areas of inquiry in a Christian's life: learning for growth in faith, for worshiping in community, and for social ministry.[42] Of course these relate to Dulles' herald, sacrament and servant models, and imply the parish community (Dulles' community and institution models) as a crucial context and environment.

Each of these three areas of inquiry is taken up in detail in the *National Catechetical Directory*. Chapter 8 on "Catechesis Toward Maturity in Faith" indicates something of the curriculum related to the first point. In this longest section of the document entitled "The Stages of Human Development," the developmental character of the life of faith is summarized and the role of catechesis at each level described:

Because the life of faith is related to human development, it passes through stages or levels; furthermore, different people possess aspects of faith to different degrees. This is true, for example, of the comprehensiveness and intensity with which God's word is accepted, of the ability to explain it, and of the ability to apply it to life. Catechesis is meant to help at each stage of human development and lead ultimately to full identification with Jesus.[43]

The task of adult education programming is one of *fostering* maturing faith, not providing it. Faith is a gift of God, fully given but received in degrees according to one's ability to respond. One's responsibility increases with growth in maturity and experience, with age and wisdom. Growth in faith is a lifelong accepting-and-learning process in a community of faith.

The second area of growth for an individual Christian is for worshiping in community. The current draft of the *National Catechetical Directory* speaks of "sacramental catechesis" both as one's preparation for participating in the sacraments and as ongoing enrichment in their meaning and implication for day to day living. Worship is integral to faith:

Faith brings the community together to worship; and in worship, faith is renewed. . . . Catechesis and liturgy are similar. Both are rooted in the Church's faith, and both, though in different ways, strengthen that faith and call Christians to conversion.[44]

Thirdly, adult learning must expand commitment

and competence in social ministry. Faith becoming
alive in awareness and worship but not in deed will die.
"By this my Father is glorified, that you bear much
fruit and so prove to be my disciples" (Jn. 15:8). This
has already become evident in the discussion of Dulles' servant model above. Adult education programming is therefore concerned about:

> . . . a twofold responsibility on the part of indi-
> viduals and the community: to strive for perfec-
> tion and give witness to Christian beliefs and val-
> ues; and to seek to correct conditions in society
> and the Church which hinder authentic human de-
> velopment and the flourishing of Christian val-
> ues.[45]

In an article published in *The Living Light* dealing
with "The Language of 'Need' in Adult Religious
Education," Maurice L. Monette argues that the curriculum and program for adult learning be the product
of a respectful dialogue between authorities and experts assessing "prescriptive needs" and learners assessing "motivational" or felt needs. Developing a
program based on prescriptive needs alone (e.g., a syl-
labus or pre-designed schema) runs the risk of learners
being indoctrinated or manipulated by education
which is not relevant or timely. Likewise, gathering
adults to identify their felt needs or interests alone is
an unsatisfactory procedure for program design because of the frequent immaturity and narrowness of
such perceived needs. Monette advocates what Freire
calls "critical reflective dialogue" around the question
"why" these needs. As teacher and student, leader

and learner, master and disciple respectfully confront the "why" of the teacher's prescriptive needs (viz., recommendations for learners) and the students' motivational needs (viz., felt needs or interests), a negotiated curriculum and program can emerge which "attempts to avoid a romantic subjectivism and individualism on the one hand and an oppressive authoritarianism on the other."[46]

The program model above suggests this relationship. The circle depicts the person as a learner in touch with felt needs. The triangle represents an agenda of prescriptive needs as suggested in this instance, by the *National Catechetical Directory*. As the circle and triangle are engaged in relationship, one within the other, a model for developing an agenda for learning becomes evident.

If the triangle provides a model for identifying a curricular frame of reference for adult lifelong learning in the parish (i.e., what authorities, experts, teachers propose as needs), it will have to be expanded until the prescriptions are specific enough to be used in dialogue. This can be accomplished when each of the three points of the triangle is expanded to three further areas of inquiry, time and again until satisfactory specificity is achieved. For the sake of exemplifying how this model can be expanded. I have developed the three categories described above one further step (see Figure 16).

Now each of these prescriptions, it is evident, can and should be further expanded with the help of whatever resources are available to us until we are satisfied that the respective triangles have become limited and tangible enough for a critical reflective dialogue. What

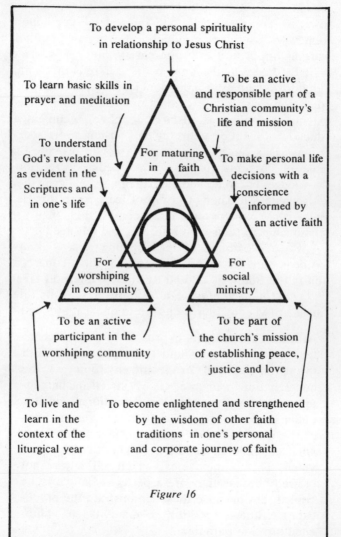

To develop a personal spirituality
in relationship to Jesus Christ

To learn basic skills in
prayer and meditation

To be an active
and responsible part of a
Christian community's
life and mission

To understand
God's revelation
as evident in the
Scriptures and
in one's life

For maturing
in faith

To make personal life
decisions with a
conscience
informed by
an active faith

For
worshiping
in community

For
social
ministry

To be an active
participant in the
worshiping community

To be part of
the church's mission
of establishing peace,
justice and love

To live and
learn in the
context of the
liturgical year

To become enlightened and strengthened
by the wisdom of other faith
traditions in one's personal
and corporate journey of faith

Figure 16

we are doing is modeling or model-building, moving toward a comprehensive and interrelated curriculum framework useful as a guideline for organizing adult learning opportunities in the parish. Since it is based on individual growth, it can be used in reference to an individual whether in individual learning, in family life education, parish family education (i.e., parish based extended families as discussed above), ecumenical education or even learning in business or social groups. This modeling process is not to provide the table of contents for an encyclopedia of religious knowledge, but to develop a map of personal growth in faith which a learner or group of learners in a parish may wish to explore more deeply and systematically in relationship to their own interests and felt needs.

The best example of this modeling process I know has been done by a United Church of Christ congregation in the South as quoted by John Westerhoff III in *Will Our Children Have Faith?* [47] Because of its relevance and vision, I have chosen to quote it at length:

> Affirming the insights expressed in the last chapter on styles of faith and the expansion of faith through interactions in specific environments, the congregation formulated clearly stated and agreed-upon aims for their church's educational ministry under the headings of *Tradition, Persons* and *Society*. Then . . . they suggested in general terms what educational experiences needed to be provided. Their conclusions, which follow, are not offered because they are a perfect example to be copied, but because they demonstrate the practical usefulness of the community of faith-enculturation paradigm.

The Tradition

Aim one: To possess a personal knowledge and understanding of God's revelation as found in the Bible, and to be disposed and able to interpret its meaning for daily individual and social life.

To achieve this aim we need: (a) To be introduced to the biblical story of God's action in history (as found in the stories of the Old and New Testaments) as *our* story; (b) to be involved in an historical, critical interpretation of the biblical story; (c) to be engaged in reflection on current social issues in the light of the biblical story.

Aim two: To possess a personal knowledge and understanding of the church's history and be disposed and able to interpret its relevance for daily individual and social life.

To achieve this aim we need: (a) To be introduced to the story of our foreparents' struggles to understand the faith and live faithfully in the world as *our* story; (b) to be involved in a critical historical investigation of the faithfulness of the institutional church throughout its history; (c) to be engaged in reflection on our contemporary striving to be a responsible and responsive community of faith in the light of our history.

Aim three: To possess a personal knowledge and understanding of the Christian faith as expressed historically in the church's creeds, cathechisms, and theological formulations; and be disposed and able to reflect theologically on contemporary life and history.

To achieve this aim we need: (a) To be provided with experiences in community which are consistent with Christian understandings of God, persons, and society; (b) to be introduced to the historic attempts of the people of God to express their faith and to engage in a critical evaluation of our contemporary expressions of faith; (c) to be engaged in reflections on contemporary life in the light of the church's historical affirmations so as to aid us in expressing our faith in meaningful ways today.

Persons

Aim four: To be committed to Jesus Christ as Lord and Savior.

To achieve this aim we need: (a) To be introduced to a community of persons who live their lives as an expression of faith in Jesus Christ as Lord and Savior; (b) to be confronted with a clear intellectual understanding of the Gospel; (c) to be provided with opportunities for a personal decision for or against the affirmation that Jesus Christ is Lord and Savior.

Aim five: To possess a personal relationship with God in Christ and to be aware of God's continual revelation.

To achieve this aim we need: (a) To have our intuitional and historical modes of consciousness enhanced and be introduced to the life of a community of meditation, prayer, and worship; (b) to be aided in our struggles of the soul and be given opportunity to experiment with various forms of meditation, prayer, and worship; (c) to be provided with opportunities to identify God's actions in contemporary history and to celebrate meaningfully in community God's past and present actions in history.

Aim six: To be a faithful and responsible member of the Christian community of faith and to share in its life and mission.

To achieve this aim we need: (a) To be offered experiences which enhance our sense of belonging to a loving, caring, affirming community of faith; (b) to be aided in building a sense of trustful, responsible relationships with others and to be provided opportunities for service in the church's life and mission; (c) to be engaged in meaningful participation in the church's life, worship, fellowship, evangelism, stewardship, service, social action, and governance.

Society

Aim seven: To be aware of our Christian vocation and be able both to make moral decisions in the light of the Christian faith and to be disposed to act faithfully and responsibly in daily individual and corporate life.

To achieve this aim we need: (a) To be provided with experiences foundational to moral decision-making, and be exposed to role models of the Christian life; (b) to be given opportunities to apply Christian faith to individual and social life;

(c) to be enabled to act and reflect faithfully and responsibly in our daily individual and corporate lives, to the end that God's kingdom comes and God's will is done.

Aim eight: To understand and be committed to the church's corporate mission in the world for justice, liberation, whole community, peace and the self-development of all peoples, and be disposed and able to engage in the continual reformation of church and society.

To achieve this aim we need: (a) To be introduced to a community of faith engaged in mission and be provided foundations for an awareness of corporate selfhood, justice, freedom, community, and peace; (b) to be given opportunity to commit one's life to social causes for the reformation of church and society; (c) to be equipped and motivated to engage in the reformation of the church and society on behalf of justice, liberation, whole community, peace, and the self-development of all people.

Aim nine: To possess an appreciative understanding of other faith traditions (Christian, Jewish, Muslim, Hindu, etc.) and to be able to enter into meaningful dialogue and action with them without sacrificing the integrity of one's own faith.

To achieve this aim we need: (a) To be exposed to persons of other faith traditions and their customs and ways; (b) to be helped to explore intellectually and experimentally the faith of other persons; (c) to be engaged in meaningful dialogue and actions with persons of other faiths.

While it is impossible to attend to specific programming models in this work,[48] I would be remiss in this section on programmatic modeling if I did not suggest a practical model for initiating and developing the need-assessment dialogue and resultant adult education programs in the local parish. This is only one of several ways to begin; I would call it an organizational or formal model of implementation since it seeks to develop the dialogue and programs "officially" in the parish, a strategy which has much to recommend it as I see the matter. The following suggestions have been adapted from the "Ten Steps in Developing Adult Program in a Y.M.C.A.," as quoted in Malcolm Knowles' *Modern Practice of Adult Education*: [49]

1. A parish discovers its concern and commitment about lifelong learning in the parish. This often occurs when some person who understands the need is able to convince others (e.g., at meetings of the parish council or its committees, at parish staff meetings, at social gatherings).

2. A member of the parish staff or pastoral team (e.g., priest, DRE, adult education director) takes official responsibility for adult education. If not full time, it is important that whatever time is given be specifically designated and carefully committed for this purpose. This person provides professional leadership and acts as executive secretary for an adult education committee. The title for this position is usually "director or coordinator of adult education."

3. The parish council or board of education recruits and commissions a standing adult education committee who is responsible to the council or board for the planning, implementation and evaluation of all

adult education activities conducted in the parish.

4. The adult education committee develops a charter, philosophy, or statement of purpose for adult education in the parish along with specific policies and guidelines.[50] Policy is most often "formulated" in dialogue between the professional (adult education director who is a member of the parish staff or pastoral team) and the lay committee members. Policy is then "adopted" by the board of education which is representative of the community, and "executed or implemented" by the director and lay people, those on the adult education committee and others. Sample policies are available for this purpose[51] and a parish may wish to call on their diocesan office for further resources and consultation in this matter.

5. A written plan is developed on the basis of a critical reflective dialogue assessing both the felt needs and interests of representative adults in relationship to the needs prescribed by authorities and experts. The committee then decides on learning activities to be made available in the parish and gives them priority in order of importance and potential effectiveness. The criterion "how many can such a program attract and involve" should not be given too great weight in this decision lest programs be limited to the low denominator of what the masses are interested in or can endure. Christ's appeal to the thousands hardly met with any success, while his work with twelve and seventy-two did.

6. These plans and programs are integrated with the rest of the pastoral plan in the parish. Hopefully, other plans in the parish have been available to the committee so that their educational components can

be included. Similarly, the committee's plans and programs are brought to the pastoral team and parish council for coordination and approval. Of course budgets and space requirements are included. The finalized statement of purpose and set of plans are also communicated to the diocesan office for information and possible coordination of specific events, resources, etc.

7. On a quarterly, semi-annual or annual basis the adult education programs are evaluated (in critical reflective dialogue) for the purpose of developing new priorities and plans. In an enterprise so expansive and complex as adult learning in faith, it is crucial that plans and programs, while not sacrificing continuity, nevertheless demonstrate spontaneity and flexibility. They need to be highly interactive with and related to both individual interests and needs as well as those of the parish as a community.

7
Issues and Challenges

The challenge of lifelong learning in the local parish, as we have seen, is a complex and demanding one. My position has been that theory is necessary for the development of this ministry, and that modeling is an effective strategy for theorizing.

As we have seen, in the modeling and theorizing process, many areas of concern need to be identified and given due attention, study and analysis. Some such critical areas of concern have been discussed above. Others have been discerned at the national level by a task force of adult education consultants to the United States Catholic Conference.[52] Convened by Brother Richard Kerressey and his successor Mr. Thomas Tewey with Fr. James Schaefer as chairman, these consultants over the past several years addressed themselves to the problems and possibilities related to adult education in the Catholic Church. In the Fall of 1977 five "critical issues" were formally identified, around which strategies for research and development are presently being considered. I share them in this context because nowhere else can we find better indicators of directions in which research and development, theorizing and modeling, need to be done relative to adult religious education.

1. The first critical issue related to adult religious education in the Catholic Church and identified by the adult education consultants is the relationship of adult learners and the "official church." Adult education principles, now commonly accepted among religious educators, describe adult learning as promotive of ever increasing self-direction and personal autonomy. This seems innocent enough until we observe what is happening to adults in our parishes, viz.,

—A majority of American Catholics feel free to ignore the Holy Father's condemnation of contraception.

—More than two-thirds expect the church will abandon its opposition to divorce, and nearly as many do not regard divorced Catholics who remarry as living in sin.

— . . . fewer than 10% of the Catholics polled believe their children would lose their souls if they left the church altogether.

—Most American Catholics are more likely to turn to prayer, to Catholic friends or to their spouse than to episcopal guidance.[53]

The dilemma, of course, is whether "the Roman Catholic Church with its tradition of authority can support an educational process which emphasizes freedom and personal self-direction."[54]

Brother Richard Kerressey who drafted the consultants' statement of this issue, suggests some directions for dealing with this issue, i.e.,

(a) reconciling on an intellectual level the theories of adult learning and the theology of developing dogma;

(b) accepting diversity in belief and practice within broad parameters of orthodoxy;

(c) recognizing that all Catholics, including ecclesial leaders, are believers and learners and teach one another with varying degrees of authority;

(d) reaffirming the principles that all Catholics are co-responsible for the governance of the church with varying degrees of authority.[55]

2. A second critical issue discerned by the adult education consultants is the complex matter of identifying how adults become more fully Christian. A kind of "taxonomy or classification" of faith development in Christian community is required. What are the processes, skills, steps, sequences and situations involved in adult personal and spiritual growth?

What little data we have points to a radical transition in American Catholicism and suggests that an institutional religion of mere externals is no longer adequate to the task. Formal and impersonal creed, code and cult (belief, morality and worship) in a mechanistic mode of experience is no longer acceptable to many American Catholics. The need for personal religious experience, and for an understanding of the dynamics and dimensions of that experience is required if such experience is to be integrated into the living stream of the church's tradition.

In 1976 Andrew Greeley, William McCready and Kathleen McCourt published a study showing a continued decline in religious devotion among Catholics. Between 1966 and 1974 the proportion of those attending weekly Mass dropped from 71% to 50%; monthly confession from 38% to 17%. Visits to a church to pray once a week declined from 23% to 15% and daily private prayer from 72% to 60%. Those attending a retreat in the preceding two years fell from 7% to 4%, making a day of recollection from 22% to 9%, making a mission from 34% to 6%.[56]

Something is awry, and Ms. Mary Good, the author of the consultants' statement on this issue, argues for the need "to analyze and to be able to utilize in adult learning the stages, needs and motivations, dynamics and processes involved in the modern adult's pilgrimage toward a fuller Christian life within the context of the Christian community," including the identification of:

(a) false assumptions about spirituality and criteria for authentic contemporary spiritualities;

(b) patterns of change and stages of development in adult life with implications for the Christian journey;

(c) the psychological models for maturing Christian persons out of which religious educators operate;

(d) the processes and dynamics engaging adult Catholics in the "movement" phenomena in American Catholicism, including Marriage Encounter, Cursillo, Better World, Charismatic, House of Prayer, etc.;

(e) learning opportunities responsive to adult

needs developed in dialogue with theologians, Biblical scholars, behavioral scientists, and adult learners themselves.[57]

3. The third critical issue facing those interested in adult learning is motivation. The challenge here, as Fr. James Schaefer puts it for the adult education consultants, is how to "develop the stimuli, challenges, and climates by which adult Catholics—laity, religious and clergy—will want freely to accept personal responsibility for their religious growth individually and for the growth of the church corporately."[58]

Evidently this motivation issue must be broached in the context of the first two issues described above; yet it takes them a step further into a consideration of some of the practical matters related to apathy and inertia. Some of the action steps suggested by Schaefer include:

(a) continued establishment and maturation of functioning pastoral and parish councils;

(b) the participation of parish, deanery and diocesan staffs and councils in workshops/ retreats wherein members can reflect upon models of church and develop the theology out of which they operate;

(c) the fostering of improved quality of liturgy in worshiping communities;

(d) the regular publication of successful programs and motivational techniques at national and diocesan levels;

(e) the contracting with a research center to analyze the dynamics and practics of motivation.[59]

4. A fourth critical issue delineated by the consultants is the development of adult education leadership. As Jane Wolford Hughes describes the issue for the consultants, "there has been a basic lack of recognition that adult education is a separate and distinctly different discipline of education." She observes that not only is there a minimal commitment of resources—time, money and facilities—in most parishes and dioceses, but also an absence of any Catholic institution which offers a graduate program in adult religious education. It goes without saying that until a significant commitment at all levels is made to the development of competent adult education leadership, adult religious education, both in terms of an educating community as described above and the educating of adults in formal programs, will remain a second class ministry in the church.[60]

The National Conference of Diocesan Directors who commissioned this work have already taken an initiative in this direction. They have funded a research project which seeks to identify competencies needed by a proficient adult education leader, as well as some resources available for their ongoing development. The project, one would hope, would stimulate graduate programs to design and implement adult education ministry or leadership programs which respond to both how and what adult learning in faith involves, and what the faith community which sponsors and nurtures that growth in faith requires in order to make this possible. The research can also be used by adult religious educators for self and peer assessment.

5. The adult education consultants outlined a fifth critical issue, the development of an adult centered church through collaboration between personnel in

adult education and leaders of movements. I would add leaders in other ministries (as discussed above) as well as movements such as Marriage Encounter, Cursillo, Charismatic and the like.

Fr. Roland Peschel, author of the consultants' position on this matter, raises the following questions:

(a) Do American Catholics see conversion as a continuing lifelong process; the necessity of faith lived in community; a shared responsibility for the church and society; the need for an integration of faith life and culture; justice as a constitutive part of Christian living?

(b) To what extent do adult religious education programs reflect and foster an adult centered church? Do adult religious education programs incorporate and follow principles of adult learning?

(c) What elements exist in the current movements in church and society to foster and hinder an adult centered church? What elements exist in the movements to lead people to be free, responsible, committed, trusting, loving persons?

(d) How can adult religious educators integrate solid principles of adult learning with the positive dynamic elements in the current movements toward nurture of an adult centered church?[61]

Peschel argues for the need to systematically identify factors, attitudes and techniques which integrate solid principles of adult learning with positive dynamic

elements in current church life, and exemplifies:
Positive factors we have observed include:

—involvement of adults in sacramental preparation programs
—opportunities for group discussion and sharing
—total family program opportunities
—use of media
—allowance and encouragement of greater reflec-
tiveness
—heightened consciousness of the need and
value of interpersonal relationships
—allowance for emotional expression
—involvement in social action
—prayer, as well as increased information and
understanding of self, others (church), God.

Some negative factors include:

—programming that is too school-modeled, i.e.,
lecture, teacher centered, regimented
—too strong sermonizing (clergy speaking at
people in liturgies)
—not allowing freedom of attendance and participation in some programs
—approaches that foster unhealthy dependency,
especially on authority, and breed fears, suspi-
cion, hostility
—poor use of media
—emphasis on prayers (words) rather than
prayer.[62]

As Tewey points out in his introduction to these

issues, they represent an effort to "discern what is emerging."

> It is from these images that we select the raw material to construct our future. It is from the inner vision that we draw strength to realize the hopes. Even as we identify issues, set goals and formulate action plans we acknowledge that while these may be powerful tools for shaping the future the deeper level of the vision, images and dreams count more.[63]

Whether we are giving expression to our visions and dreams in theoretical models or translating them into action with experimental models, it is the future we seek to affect. These issues indicate some of the most demanding and immanent challenges we now face. All of them relate intimately to lifelong learning in the local parish, and all of them are the subject for much in the way of future research and development.

Notes

1. Hans Kung, *The Church*, (New York: Sheed and Ward, 1967), p. 85.

2. James R. Schaefer directs attention to this distinction between "contexual" and "programmatic" approaches in "Update on Adult Education in Churches and Synagogues, II Roman Catholicism," *Religious Education*, LXXII, No. 2, March-April, 1977, pp. 133–143.

3. For a more complete discussion of this matter see Ian G. Barbour, *Myths, Models and Paradigms —A Comparative Study in Science and Religion*, (New York: Harper and Row, 1974).

4. See for example David Tracy's *Blessed Rage for Order —The New Pluralism in Theology*, (New York: The Seabury Press, 1975).

5. Barbour, *Myths*, p. 50.

6. See Gordon L. Lippitt, *Visualizing Change —Model Building and the Change Process*, (La Jolla, Calif.: University Associates, Inc., 1973).

7. Malcolm Knowles, *The Adult Learner: A Neglected Species*, (Houston: Gulf Publishing Company, 1973), pp. 92–93.

8. Avery Dulles, S.J., *Models of the Church —A Critical Assessment of the Church in All Its Aspects*, (Garden City, N.Y.: Doubleday and Company, Inc., 1974).

9. Some of the finest commentary on these models is found in Vatican II's Constitution of the Church, *Lumen Gentium*, Chapter 2 (community) and 3 (institution). See Austin Flannery (ed.), *Vatican Council II*, (Northport, N.Y.: Costello Publishing Company), pp. 359–387.

10. For excellent bibliographies relative to each of these models see the notes in Dulles, *op. cit.*, pp. 193–207. I do not find it appropriate in this context to broach other systems and

models, e.g., those of Congar, Rahner, Kung, McBrien, Baum, Gutierrez, Kilian, Theisen and others.

11. See the five volume series by Juan Luis Segundo, *A Theology for Artisans of a New Humanity*, (Maryknoll, N.Y.: Orbis Books) and Gustavo Gutierrez, *A Theology of Liberation*, (Maryknoll, N.Y.: Orbis Books, 1973).

12. "The Church in the Modern World" is a superb Vatican II statement on this model. See Flannery, *op. cit.*, pp. 903–1014.

13. Richard P. McBrien, *The Remaking of the Church—An Agenda for Reform*, (New York: Harper and Row, 1973), pp. 71–136.

14. Morton Kelsey, *Can Christians Be Educated?* (Mishawaka, Ind.: Religious Education Press, Inc., 1977), pp. 110–111.

15. The best popular work of which I am aware that deals with the mechanistic and organismic world views is Malcolm Knowles, *The Adult Learner*, (Minneapolis, Minn.: Bethany Fellowship, Inc., 1972).

16. Wayne Rood, *Understanding Christian Education*, (Nashville, Tenn.: Abingdon Press, 1970).

17. See Stanley Krippner, *Song of the Siren—A Parapsychological Odyssey*, (New York: Harper and Row, 1975), pp. 40–45.

18. See George B. Leonard, *Education and Ecstasy*, (New York: Dell Publishing Company, 1968).

19. Flannery, *op. cit.*, "The Church in the Modern World," par. 14, p. 915.

20. Douglas McGregor, *The Human Side of Enterprise*, (New York: McGraw-Hill, 1960).

21. Abraham Maslow, *The Farther Reaches of Human Nature*, (New York: Viking Press, 1971).

22. See note 2 above.

23. John H. Westerhoff III, *Will Our Children Have Faith?* (New York: Seabury Press), pp. 49–50.

24. *National Catechetical Directory*, (Draft for the "Modi" of the Bishops), par. 30.

25. Robert R. Blake and Jane S. Mouton, *Grid Organization Development*, (Reading, Pa.: Addison-Wesley Publishing Co., 1969) and *Consultation*, (Reading, Pa.: Addison-

Wesley Publishing Co., 1976). This excellent resource for leaders contains an instrument which assists the reader to develop a personal Leader Effectiveness and Adaptability Description (LEAD)" and assess ones preferred styles and degree of flexibility. I highly recommend it as a primary resource for the training of leaders in the local parish.

26. See William R. Lassey and Richard R. Fernandez, (ed.), *Leadership and Social Change*, (La Jolla, Calif.: University Associates, Inc., 1976).

27. See Paul Hersey and Kenneth H. Blanchard, *Management of Organizational Behavior: Utilizing Human Resources*, (Englewood Cliffs, N. J.: Prentice-Hall, Inc., 1977).

28. In the Diocese of Orlando Bishop Thomas Grady has issued a superb goal statement in the name of (and after broad consultation with) the people of the diocese. This serves as a beacon for growth and development in the diocese. See "A Statement of Diocesan Pastoral Priorities," *Origins*, Vol. 6, pp. 688 ff.

29. We have developed a "Models of the Church" Workshop as a method of setting goals. See "A Workshop Design in Ecclesiology," *Pace 5*, (Winona, Minn.: St. Mary's College Press, 1974).

30. Uri Merry and Melvin Allerhand, *Developing Teams and Organizations*, (Reading, Mass.: Addison-Wesley Publishing Co., 1977).

31. For an excellent instrument to assist pastoral teams assess their relationship and effectiveness, see the "Group Effectiveness Survey" in David A. Nadler, *Feedback and Organization Development: Using Data-Based Methods*, (Reading, Mass.: Addison-Wesley Publishing Co., 1977), pp. 194–198.

32. W. J. Reddin, *Effective Management by Objectives—The 3-D Method of MBO*, (New York: McGraw-Hill Book Company, 1971).

33. See George M. Prince, *The Practice of Creativity Through Synectics—The Proven Method of Group Problem-Solving*, (New York: Collier Books, 1970).

34. See Jay Galbraith, *Designing Complex Organizations*, (Reading, Mass.: Addison-Wesley Publishing Co., 1973).

35. See Speed Leas and Paul Kittlaus, *Church Fights — Managing Conflict in the Local Church*, (Philadelphia, Pa.: The Westminster Press, 1973).

36. These distinctions and considerations to follow are adopted from Malcolm Knowles, *The Modern Practice of Adult Education*, (New York: Association Press, 1970), p. 62.

37. Malcolm Knowles, *The Adult Learner*, p. 97.

38. *National Catechetical Directory*, par. 32.

39. Gabriel Moran, *Religious Body*, (New York: Seabury Press, 1974).

40. Loretta Girzaitis, *The Church as Reflecting Community—Models of Adult Religious Learning*, (West Mystic, Conn.: Twenty-Third Publications, 1977), p. 20.

41. Malcolm Knowles, *The Adult Learner*, pp. 173–176.

42. See *National Catechetical Directory*, Chapters 6, 7, and 8.

43. *Ibid.*, par. 172.

44. *Ibid.*, par. 110–111.

45. *Ibid.*, par. 38.

46. Maurice L. Monette, "The Language of 'Need' in Adult Religious Education," in manuscript.

47. See John Westerhoff III, *op. cit.* pp. 105–109.

48. Some such models are described in Loretta Girzaitis, *The Church*, pp. 55–162.

49. Knowles, *Modern Practice*, pp. 74–76.

50. The theoretical discussion above is helpful background material for the committee as well as many of the resources mentioned in the notes.

51. See *Giving Form to the Vision*, (Washington: National Catholic Education Association, 1974), pp. 21–34.

52. This group of consultants, chaired by Rev. James Schaefer, has included: Sr. Marie Agnew, Sr. Diana Bader, Sr. Leonard Donvan, Dr. Thomas A. Downs, Rev. John J. Flattery, Ms. Loretta Girzaitis, Ms. Mary Good, Msgr. Norbert J. Henry, Mr. Peter L. Houck, Mrs. Jane Wolford Hughes, Rev. Robert L. Kinast, Dr. Laurence J. Losoncy, Rev. Roland A. Peschel, Sr. Maureen Shanghnessy, Rev. Jacques Weber.

53. "Has the Church Lost Its Soul," *Newsweek*, Oct. 4, 1971, pp. 80–89.

54. From an unpublished report of the adult education consultants edited by Thomas Tewey, of the USCC, November, 1977.

55. *Ibid.*

56. Andrew M. Greeley, William C. McCready, Kathleen McCourt, *Catholic Schools in a Declining Church*, (Kansas City: Sheed and Ward, Inc., 1976), pp. 28–31.

57. Tewey, (ed.), Consultants Report.

58. *Ibid.*

59. *Ibid.*

60. *Ibid.*

61. *Ibid.*

62. *Ibid.*

63. *Ibid.*